Life Wants to Live
Real Stories of Tibetan Refugees

This collection of testimonies tells the heart-wrenching and inspiring stories of Tibetan exiles living as refugees in India.

The tales were originally told to Paola Martani as she researched her thesis in the Himalayan mountains: a place where she lived for years as a local - wearing silk and wool, drinking tea with butter, learning the language, religion, and mythology.

In the pages of the book Martani shares her experiences in this spiritually rich land as well as sharing the stories of the remarkable individuals she encountered there. From a world coexistent but different from any other, from a dimension of unreality, she has assembled the gestures and discoverd the cadences and secrets that from the true essence of this work.

From the tragedy of the reality, she has realized that life is precious, if not for you, then for itself. She has discovered that, despite everthing. life wants to live.

Life Wants to Live
Real Stories of Tibetan Refugees

Foreword by HH the XIV Dalai Lama

PAOLA MARTANI

STERLING PUBLISHERS (P) LTD.
Regd. Office: A1/256 Safdarjung Enclave,
New Delhi-110029. CIN: U22110DL1964PTC211907
Phone: +91 82877 98380
e-mail: mail@sterlingpublishers.in
www.sterlingpublishers.in

Life Wants to Live: Real Stories of Tibetan Refugees
© 2019, Paola Martani
ISBN 978 93 86245 61 8

Cover designed by Sayanti Bhattacharya.

All rights are reserved.
No part of this publication may be reproduced, stored in a retrieval system or transmitted, in any form or by any means, mechanical, photocopying, recording or otherwise, without prior written permission of the publisher.

Printed and Published in India by
Sterling Publishers Pvt. Ltd.,
Plot No. 13, Ecotech-III, Greater Noida -201306, U.P. India

Dedication

I dedicate these pages to His Holiness the Fourteenth Dalai Lama of Tibet, Tenzin Gyatso, with the prayer that he will return to this world, again and again as long as there are sentient beings trapped in samsara, and with the hope that in this life he will live long and will be able to return to Lhasa.

I dedicate this work to the Three Jewels—the Buddha, the Dharma, and the Sangha. By the merits I have gained thanks to the practise of generosity and the other perfections, may I obtain the status of a Buddha for the benefit of all sentient beings.

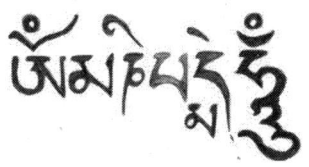

THE DALAI LAMA

FOREWORD

Tibet has a rich cultural heritage, a fine language, and a long history. The tradition of Buddhism in Tibet, introduced by Shantarakshita, an eminent scholar of the ancient Indian monastic university of Nalanda, relies heavily on reason and logic. As Buddhist teachings contain a wealth of knowledge on the workings of the mind and emotions, they remain highly relevant today.

Although Tibetans in Tibet have been through so much suffering and tragedy, they have managed to keep their culture, language and identity alive. Many died resisting Communist China's suppressive policies, while others continue to suffer. Some were able to escape into exile and have shared their stories with the outside world. Accounts of their suffering are recorded in many books, articles, and documentary films.

Dr. Paola Martani, an Italian national, has recorded in her book, *Life Wants to Live*, the accounts of Tibetan political prisoners. She also relates the efforts being made toward a reconciliatory and mutually beneficial solution to the Tibetan issue.

22 February 2019

Acknowledgments

First and foremost, my thanks go to His Holiness the Fourteenth Dalai Lama, Tenzin Gyatso, and to the karma that has allowed me to be in his presence so many times, that has placed my hands in his and granted me his blessings, for the embrace that removed the tearing pain that I carried in my heart for far too long. To him, I give boundless thanks.

I am also deeply indebted to His Holiness the Seventeenth Karmapa, for having granted, the inexperienced young girl that I was, an interview, and for the kindness that will remain forever embedded in my memory.

My thanks also go to Ngawang Sonam, translator to His Holiness the Dalai Lama, for the bond of friendship between us, the spiritual support that has guided me in the difficult moments of my life, for his belief and trust in me in the assignments which even today I feel I would not have been able to carry out otherwise. Thanks also to Ngawang Migmar, the little-great man, whose affection and dedication will always be a part of me; to Tsering Wangdue, an elder brother who, while I was taking my first steps in the Tibetan community, never ceased to encourage me, helping me with translation and finding my feet in a new culture; to Thutop Gyaltsen, my little brother who is almost starting his adult life, who is close to me even when physically far away; to Karma Ringzin and Passang

Dolma, my jewels, who have been my strength and my love, and this will never change; and to Max, who has been my family from Italy.

My gratitude goes to my grandmother and also to the people of Tibet, who have welcomed me, taught me the meaning of contentment, and offered me a piece of their lives without even a hint of egoism. I thank you for the strength that you have given me, and for sharing with me the most beautiful secret—whatever happens, life wants to live.

Preface

In 2012, with a big dream, a lot of courage, and a suitcase in hand, I hugged my family goodbye, and left Italy. I boarded a plane, thinking that in two months I would be flying back home. I travelled overnight towards the east. In my long, black skirt I got acquainted with the heat of New Delhi in the few hours of transit, before flying to the north.

One hour and thirty minutes later, there I was, in a taxi that sped towards the sky—the blue sky of the high Himalayan mountains. I found myself immersed in shaved heads, red and yellow clothes, and long black braids.

The monasteries created a small dream. The air was cool and steeped in mystery. I kept the suitcase in an apartment located just beyond a small forest. There were the monkeys, the cows, and the shock of the impact of something so vastly different.

I was 22, and in the first six months of my stay in Dharamsala, I wrote stories I gathered from the lives of the people who gave me accommodation. The two months I thought I would stay became six, and then another six. I was unable to get my fill of the new sounds, the gestures, the mystery and the secrets that were unveiled, little by little, while I was learning to understand a new language. I learned to kneel in temples, to circumambulate around them clockwise; I dressed in a silk chupa, the traditional costume of the Tibetan people, making peace between Italian simplicity and Tibetan embroidery. I started to appreciate turquoise and coral jewellery and to recognize the unobtainable precious dzi stones from the thousands of fakes that can be found on roadside. I taught my taste buds to get used to the different, rural tastes of barley flour, *tsampa*, and dry yak's cheese— *chura*. I loved, and I found love, in the simple power of the traditions that have been preserved through time, never changing, despite all the external stimuli that urged them towards 'evolution'.

I found a household in those Indian mountains whose members presented themselves as if they were Tibetans in Tibet, a symbol full of hope to maintain their identity and not to let it die. I found family in an adopted brother—in his smile, in his sweetness, in his courage to have grown up alone, a little man in his eighth year; in a younger brother, who had arrived in India at the beginning of his adolescence, who is still fighting today to reconcile his nature with the need to adapt to a world so different from where he grew up; in a man who shared with me a special bond and who, after two years, is always ready to lend a helping hand in times of trouble. I found a family in two children, at the time too small to go to school, who are today almost my match in height and surely wiser than I myself can sometimes be. In two-and-a-half years, I was taught that everything that happens to me has been created by me; that killing even a mosquito is an action that will bring pain; that kindness of the heart is the only weapon that will prevail in any field.

I spent months among people who were living as refugees in a land that is not theirs, who had lived through hell and fought tooth-and-nail not to forget, not to get lost. And I, in order not to lose them due to the distance that is now three years from these memories, reopen a dissertation that I presented in February 2014 in Statale di Milano University. I opened it and decided to rewrite it, now that I am in Delhi, now that the snow-covered peaks and the peace of the mountains are only an echo in my mind while I live in the chaotic traffic of the capital of India, now that the simplicity of that world is a bigger contrast with the complexity of the environment of embassies, the simplicity that intoxicates me and flows through my veins. I reopened the thesis and, at the right distance to analyse the situation, I decided to rewrite it as a book, in order not to forgot, in order not to lose hold of the past.

Contents

Dedication	5
Foreword	7
Acknowledgements	9
Preface	11
• A Little History	17
• Wandu	27
• Dicky	36
• Ven. Bagdro	40
• Renewal	57
• Gu-Chu-Sum	63
• Phuntsok Wangdu	69
• Zomkyi	83
• Sonam Dicky	91
• LT	97
• Visual Testimonies	110
• Future Memories	112
• Tenzin Lhaky	119
• Milarepa	122
• Thang Tong Gyalpo	125
• Tenzin Lhaky	127
• Burning in the Fire	133

- Tenzin Tsundue   135
- His Holiness the Seventeenth Karmapa   142
- Conclusion   146
- Bibliography   152

A Little History

Tibet is called the 'altar of the earth'.[1] Its territory covers 2,500,000 square kilometres and is defended by the Himalayan barrier to the south, by river-carved gorges to the east, and by desolate plains to the north and west.

Twelve centuries ago, it was a land of tribes, ruled by warrior kings who strove to make offerings to the gods of the earth and tried to find a means of communication with the afterlife. These same kings, after the introduction of Buddhism, turned into defenders of inner peace, convinced that if humans sought to understand themselves, they could get rid of negative trends and develop unlimited positivity, acquiring real happiness.

After a thousand years of Buddhism, in the 17th century, the monasteries began to assume the responsibilities of government. The king had no natural descendants and this led the people to see reincarnation (the belief that a person can be re-born into a different body after death) as a vehicle for succession.

The Dalai Lama[2] assumed the role of a temporal and spiritual leader, being considered an emanation of the Buddha of compassion—*Avalokiteshvara*.

---

1. Altar of the Earth: Tibet is located at 5,000 metres above sea-level.
2. Dalai Lama literally means 'Ocean of Wisdom'. The Dalai Lama is the highest theocrat of the Tibetan people. He is the head of the *Guleg* school of Tibetan Buddhism and, from the mid-600 until 1959, was the absolute ruler of Tibet.

Many Buddhist universities were founded in order to help people reach enlightenment. The desire for enlightenment radiates throughout Tibetan culture, starting with the observation of the relationship between these people and the divine—there is no belief in a god, especially one that created the world to punish them; in Tibet there is no concept of a god who exercises power over people. Instead, the belief that happiness depends on transforming one's mind and one's own actions is predominant.

Tibet remained isolated from the rest of the world until the early 20th century. After that time, however, the English and Chinese made incursions into Tibetan territory, and in 1912, the thirteenth Dalai Lama[3] felt the need to declare independence. This decision was also motivated by the growing difficulties that the Buddhists of Mongolia were facing at that time with China.

The Dalai Lama tried to strengthen the army, but he was not able to do it because of the increasing opposition of conservative monks. Before he passed away, he left a warning—We have to defend ourselves from the red communists, otherwise they will attack the heart of Tibet, its religion, and government, the monasteries will be destroyed and the monks expelled. Everything will collapse in fear and we will suffer a great pain.

---

3. Thubten Gyatso (born 12th February, 1876, died 17th December, 1933) was the Thirteenth Dalai Lama of Tibet. To this day he is referred as *The Great Thirteenth*.

In 1949, Chairman Mao[4] founded the Peoples' Republic of China (PRC). His first action on an international level was the 'liberation' of Tibet, which began around 1950, officialised by the Battle of Chamdo, where the so-called 'peaceful liberation of Tibet' officially took place.

The Tibetans had no idea what 'liberation' meant in the political sphere. They found themselves liberated, but they were not sure from what. For them the word liberation was a spiritual concept that entailed an escape from the sufferings of the material world, obtainable through wisdom and compassion. Their concept could not have been more different than what this term meant in the communist dictionary—the subversion by the oppressive economic system.

There was no question of the Tibetan army being able to match the Chinese troops in Lhasa. The Chinese government installed itself in the capital without much difficulty. The fourteenth Dalai Lama[5]—15 years old at the time and motivated by the desire to alleviate the effects of the Chinese occupation on his people—tried to reach a compromise with the invaders, motivated by the desire to alleviate the effects of the Chinese occupation on his people. Initially, the government in Beijing took control only of international affairs and

---

4. Chairman Mao, also called Mao Tse-tung or Mao Zedong (Shaonshan, 26th December, 1893–Beijing, 9th September, 1976) was a Chinese revolutionary and dictator. Spokesman of the Chinese Communist Party from 1943 until his death, he was the president of the People's Republic of China, which was founded in 1949. During his leadership of China, he developed a Chinese version of Marxism–Leninism, known as Maoism, collectivizing agriculture.

5. At the age of two, the child Lhamo Dondrub (born 6th July, 1935) was recognized as the Fourteenth Dalai Lama, Tenzin Gyatso.

promised to leave intact the political and religious institutions of Tibet.

In 1954, the top two Tibetan leaders (the Dalai Lama and the Panchen Lama[6]) went to Beijing, motivated by the idea that communist ideals of equality could be reconciled with Buddhist ones—a hope that was shattered by Mao's proclamation, 'Religion is poison'.

The illusion of a possible collaboration with the new people was not present only in the political sphere—even the Chinese army referred to themselves as 'guests' in Tibet. After the Tibetan army surrendered, there was no looting and the land was redistributed to the peasants. The problems began when it came to the villages whose lands were the property of the monasteries, where a policy of attack on the religion was inaugurated in accordance with the slogan, 'Religion is fraud; it doesn't exist. Neither do God nor spirits.' Fear among Tibetan people began to rise, as the teachings of the Buddha were their main paths for living.

In March 1959, the situation became explosive, thanks to the testimonies of refugees who brought evidence to Lhasa of how Chinese policy had changed. To arm themselves and fight was against the vow of the monastic, but they began to violate this constraint in order to defend Dharma. The Dalai Lama himself was aware that the people would give their lives to defend Dharma. Disguised as a Chinese soldier, the Dalai Lama

---

6. The Panchen Lama was the second-most important lamaistic position in Tibet until the 1950s.

escaped from the capital to avoid a massacre.[7] A few days after his departure, his Norbulingha palace was bombed. The subsequent protests by the Tibetans were used as the reason to suppress all forms of resistance.

In 1960, the International Commission of Jurists, an organization for the defence of human rights, stated that China was guilty of genocide in Tibet. American interest in the Tibetan cause began in the 1950s— Tibetan soldiers were trained for mountain warfare. The resistance, with this help, went on for ten years. America, in 1960, decided on a change of course. Putting an end to their help of the Tibetan people, they created an alliance with China to face Soviet power.

Many soldiers killed themselves, having vowed not to give up.

In 1966, the Cultural Revolution began. A movement that involved the whole of China, it was designed to destroy the past, considered a source of backwardness.

Tibet was brutalized by this exercise. Six thousand monasteries were destroyed, their treasures looted and taken to China, and the holy Buddhist canons were burnt. The Tibetan language, the religious language of the past, was prohibited and replaced with Chinese— the language of 'progress'. Tibetans were downgraded to second-class citizens, based on the evidence that they could not follow school lessons (the monthly fee of a school exceeded—and still often exceeds—the annual income of a Tibetan family). The Chinese travel

---

7. To understand a Tibetan, it is necessary to understand what the Dalai Lama means to them. A Christian who anticipates the second coming of the Messiah may best liken it to this—for a Tibetan, the equivalent of the Messiah is always present in this life, represented by the figure of His Holiness the Dalai Lama.

to Tibet to exploit the economic resources, thanks to government incentives, but do not consider Tibetans as compatriots.

In 1976, Mao died. The nightmare that lasted ten years, the Cultural Revolution, was over.

The new Chinese leadership briefly showed an interest in meeting the Dalai Lama. There was the illusion of a possible reconciliation. This glimmer of hope was soon extinguished. By the order of the Dalai Lama, three delegates of the Tibetan Government-in-exile left for Tibet. While they travelled through the country, they found crowds screaming and pleading with them to report to His Holiness the brutalities that were happening.

Since then, the Dalai Lama has travelled the world, spreading Buddhist teachings. He has adopted a policy of compassion toward the Chinese, weakened by their own actions, which has led them to lose their humanity.[8]

In 1987, during the committee conference on human rights in Washington, the Dalai Lama proposed peace through a Five Point Peace Plan to resolve the issue of Tibet. Tibet would accept the compromise to remain under the supervision of the Peoples' Republic of China in matters of foreign affairs and defence, but it demanded internal autonomy.

China rejected this plan, and also opposed the international travel of the representative of the government-in-exile, considering their meetings with officials of other countries unacceptable.

---

8. Quote: 'Whenever I see beings that are wicked in nature and overwhelmed by violent negative actions and suffering, I shall hold such rare ones dear, as if I had found a precious treasure' —*Eight Verses on Mind Training*.

Tibet, to confirm Chinese occupation, still hosts 300,000 Chinese soldiers. Control of this land allows China to exercise hegemony over all the Asian countries. It is, after all, a land full of natural resources, with a great strategic value, being the heart of Asia and managing its entire water sources.

In 1989, after having pursued a policy of non-violence for many years, the Dalai Lama was awarded the Nobel Peace Prize.

After this recognition, there were demonstrations in Chinese territory (by students) calling for freedom. All the protests were suppressed for fear that they would bring a feeling of disruption in people's minds.

In 1995, the Dalai Lama identified a six-year-old child as the reincarnation of the Panchen Lama. A few days after the announcement, the child and his family disappeared, becoming political prisoners. In his place, Beijing installed a child of its own choice.[9] The Chinese Government has never allowed any international agency to verify whether the missing child is still alive or not.

The Chinese have always seen Tibet as part of their sphere of influence. This belief is reinforced by the fact that in the times of difficulty, Tibet has requested the support of Chinese troops. Actually, the irrefutable fact that is opposed to this interpretation is that the Tibetan language is distinctly different from Mandarin. Their

---

9. According to tradition, when the Dalai Lama dies, the Panchen Lama, Reting Rinpoche, and other eminent monks initiate investigations to find his reincarnation using oracles and interpreting dreams and omens. Once the reincarnation is identified, usually as a very young child, he is consecrated and enthroned officially, beginning his novice study, but until he reaches his majority, executive power is exercised by a regent.

politics and currency differ, as does the spirit to defend their way of life.

The colonization of Tibet is a recent phenomenon and yet most people see it as a remote happening. This has probably led the West to close its eyes to the many examples of violations of human rights—the Chinese re-colonization of Tibet, in fact, was a real ethnic cleansing. A Tibetan cannot speak openly about his or her distinctive nationality or in praise of their leader, the Dalai Lama, in their own land as they would end up in jail.

The main crop in Tibet was barley; Mao, during the Cultural Revolution (1966–76), ordered farmers to plant wheat, preferred in China, but totally unsuited to the harsh Tibetan climate. Over the next two decades, 50 per cent of the population died of starvation in the resulting famine. Data indicates that one in six Tibetans died as a result of the Chinese policies imposed in the country. Lhasa, the capital, which literally means 'place of the gods', is now home to a one-and-a-half square kilometre red-light district for the fun of the Chinese troops, and the city is being rebuilt in the Chinese style, while entire Tibetan neighbourhoods are torn down.

The development of Tibet thus proves to be a double-edged sword. On the one hand it is necessary; on the other, as long as it is ruled by Chinese policy, there will be no benefit to Tibetan people, but only result in political and cultural repression. Tibetans have no access to any political role and cannot contribute to the economy. They have no freedom, even within their monasteries, which are run by a Chinese office that prohibits not only the worship of His Holiness the Dalai Lama, but also keeping a picture of him.

In 1996, China began the so-called *Iron Fist Campaign* on a national scale. In Tibet, it was directed at separatists. Monks who swore allegiance to the Dalai Lama were imprisoned and mass executions took place in public, to discourage all acts of pro-independence.

Hunger strikes were repeatedly staged by youth in order to draw attention to the Tibetan situation. Less frequent, but much more disturbing, were the self-immolations—desperate and unimaginable acts of protest in which a human being sets fire to their own body achieving, death after endless hours of pain.

Despite terrible torture, the Buddhist teaching was so ingrained in the Tibetans that they still have not broken[10] their commitment to non-violence even after nearly 59 years of struggle against the Chinese rule.

In order that their future generations continue their struggle, schools have been founded in exile, to educate their younger generations and continue their struggle for the peaceful resolution of the Tibetan issue. These schools have been established to raise Tibetan children with a traditional Tibetan upbringing, while also ensuring that they receive a good, modern education.

In the past, every year, around three thousand Tibetans would risk their lives trying to cross borders and get to India after months of travelling.[11] Now China has literally made escape impossible for the Tibetans

---

10. Quote: 'They may torture my body but not my soul'—Palden Gyatso, the Tibetan monk who spent 33 years in China before fleeing to Dharamsala where he wrote the book *The Fire Under the Snow*.

11. Quote: 'We do not fight for a piece of land but for a way of life, culture, and civilization that teaches us to consider life and every human being the most precious of treasures.'

by closing all borders to Nepal, only allowing those who have licenses for trade to travel back and forth. After years in India, after months in New Tibet, I know that everything is pure non-permanence, evolving. After hours of breathing the smell of melted butter and incense, hours filling my eardrums with the almost mystical sounds of trumpets and hoarse voices repeating mantras,[12] I know that nothing is fixed and everything changes.

There was a time when no one could have conceived of the fall of the Berlin Wall, or of a Russia different from the Soviet Union. These things once seemed unattainable events. There was a time when the moon seemed like a dream, untouchable. Maybe you just have to believe, maybe anything can happen.

In these dark times, even if the situation is difficult, I still believe in a peaceful solution to the issue of Tibet. After all these years of pain, the hope of being free is still not lost; while the Western world explores space out there, we explore the inner space.

—His Holiness the Fourteenth Dalai Lama

---

12. Mantras are prayers which consist of syllables chosen to make some soul ropes vibrate (repeated 108 times to form a complete prayer). These are often words in Sanskrit which are blessed and have significant impact if you recite them with complete devotion.

Wandu

We are sitting together outside the guest house of the Tibetan Children's Village (TCV) of Suja. We are waiting for my children to finish their day at school so I can finally embrace them. We are talking about different topics, our conversation interspersed with minutes of silence—a vacuum of words that does not bother us. We are friends, we have a strong bond. He is a brother with different blood from mine, an adopted brother. We share all emotions and thoughts without fear of judgment—we are totally free from any pretence and this makes us light, as light as the scene taking shape in front of us—endless green fields, surrounded only by white peaks.

I feel great affection for this person and I know he feels the same about me. There are no secrets, even the most hidden ones are revealed.

On this day in late June, he decides to let other people know his thoughts, through my words. He looks at me, inviting me to take up my notebook and pen, a blue ink pen, and says, 'Take notes of everything and then write my story.'

My name is Wandu. I was born in central Tibet in 1987. I do not know the exact day nor the month, but I'm almost certain about the year.

My mother is a housewife, my father has a small business. I have a younger brother. He in Tibet. He works there. How could a mother conceive of losing both of her children? This is my only comfort when, watching a child in its parent's arms, I hold tight to the memory of what it's like to have one's parents next door. It is a good consolation when I would wonder why it is just I among all the members of my family who has this Indian destiny.

I remember little about my childhood. I know that weeks passed, far from home, in the company of a strict teacher who had banned sports and games and was teaching me Chinese.

I knew nothing of my country at that time. I did not know which part of my people had opted for the path of separation. No one talked about it, especially in the town—too many soldiers, too afraid.

I decided to come to India on my own, though I was not really conscious of the decision. One day they asked me if I wanted to go to that land, where there are so many cars and fruit stands everywhere. 'Yes!' was my answer, but I said it only because at that time I wanted to escape from my teacher and the endless school rules.

I was almost eight years old when, one early morning, I bade farewell to my parents, not knowing that I would never meet them again, probably never in this life. I thought it was a holiday, a little trip before returning to those four walls where I could experience the comfort of my family.

I had company on the way—a dozen other kids about my age, between seven and ten years old. On the first three days we were packed tightly in a truck, without the possibility of seeing the light of the sun. We stopped at the edge of a desert. From there, we would have to go the rest of the way on foot. The only moment I clearly remember, impregnated by spirit emotions, by sensations of touch and sight, was when we were crossing the mountain Shar Gang La or Nangpala Pass, which separates Tibet from Nepal. I remember that the pass was virtually a wall of mountain with snow everywhere and it was extremely cold. That was my first-hand experience which taught me that, at such a high altitude with snow everywhere, it is almost impossible to open your eyes without wearing some kind of protection. Without protection, you could go blind for several days, if lucky, and if not, then you could become blind for life.

I remember my blindness lasted weeks. I went through a phase when it was dark everywhere I looked. It took days for the white halos to become clear, regain thickness and return to colour.

I had no prior knowledge of the risk that I exposed myself to—blindness, jail, death and so on. I was completely ignorant. It's good that I didn't know, because later I began to understand the terrible experiences others had to go through, and the fear that still haunted them.

Once in Nepal, luck turned against us several times. The Nepalese police at Solu Khumbu received us only to send us back to the Tibetan border. However, we managed to find some place in the forest to hide from the police, and then later a bus to take us to Kathmandu, the capital of Nepal. Upon our arrival at Kathmandu, we were again captured and kept in captivity until, with the help of the Tibetan Reception Centre (TRC) there, we were released and given shelter in the TRC, one of the units of the Tibetan Administration-in-exile.

After staying together in the Tibetan Reception Centre for some time, I had to say goodbye to my travel companions. Although I really wished I could join them and go to India, I couldn't. I had serious knee ailments that kept me stranded in Nepal for another three months. When I finally recovered completely, I made the three-day journey to Delhi in a bus with a family—a father and his two sons. After spending a night in Delhi, I boarded a night bus to Dharamsala and, finally, I reached my ultimate destination.

It was October 1995 when, after ten days at the Reception Centre[13] in Dharamsala, I had an audience with His Holiness the Dalai Lama. At that time I had no idea what His Holiness looked like. I had only heard people calling His Holiness' name and praying when they were overwhelmed with grief and fear, and during difficult times. In the past, I used to think he was not real. I thought that his name was one of the many mythical names that people used to call upon when in distress.

That day my mother's words ran through my mind, words she spoke while she was fixing my jacket for the last time before I left for my new life. 'Do not be sad, you will have the honour of being blessed by His Holiness'—words which were meaningless until, sitting among the new Tibetans in India, I saw a man dressed in red coming towards me. To see him arriving was to see a dream come true—the living Buddha was moving towards me, becoming more and more real, warming my heart with every step he took towards me. I could not look into his eyes. My god, a god that no one ever told me was real, was actually talking to me!

In November, I started school at TCV, which is quite close to McLeod Ganj, the residential town of His Holiness the Dalai Lama. I had to attend a special class called Opportunity Class as I started my school rather late. At school, I lived at Home No. 16, which had about 30 children of different ages

---

13. The Department of Security of the Tibetan Government-in-exile runs three Reception Centres to look after the growing number of new refugees from Tibet. The refugees usually arrive in Nepal from where they go to Dharamsala and other Tibetan communities, via Delhi. There are branches of Reception Centres in Kathmandu and Delhi, where new refugees are given food and lodging and guided to their onward destinations. The Reception Centre also helps new refugees to find jobs and join schools and monasteries.

who became my new brothers and sisters. Each home has a stepmother to look after the children. After a two-month attendance at the Opportunity Class, the school broke-off for its two months of winter holidays. Those holidays were hard, the hardest of all for me. When other children from around India and Nepal went home, those of us from Tibet and other orphans were left back at the school. At that time, I missed my parents very much. I began a life where I had to live without any parents to look up to for protection and direction, warmth, and care. Although there were other children like me at school to spend time with, I always felt lonesome during the winter holidays.

At school in exile, since the age of eight, I grew up taking care of myself. I learnt to wash my few clothes by my own hands. I was poor to the point that I could not afford to buy anything. Except the three meals that were provided to us daily at school, I had nothing to eat like other children who had parents to pamper them with sweets and presents. Like me, all others left behind at school during the winter holiday were also penniless.

In January 1996, I began attending class 2, but I still did not know how to read or write.

As time passed, I slowly began to understand the fate of my country, its culture and history.

We are different from the Chinese, racially, linguistically, history, culturally, and geographically. Slowly, I began to understand why we were fighting for our right to live freely on our own land.

Growing up in Tibet under the Chinese rule is different from growing in a purely Tibetan environment. I spent eight years of my life in Tibet, standing by, unable to learn the traditions and culture that I was supposed to learn naturally from my parents. For eight years I lived *a life which was under the shadow of ignorance and fear. In Tibet, under the Chinese, cigarettes, alcohol, and prostitution were easily available with no restriction, and were easily accessible at an early age. This hasn't changed to this date. This is in sharp contrast to our normal way of life as Tibetans. We are a Buddhist people and for us these acts contaminate life and ruin the spirit, create bad karma and ensure for us an undesirable destiny in the next life.*

When I was at home in Tibet, we were taught basic communist ideas. Although I had heard them over and over again, I didn't really understand the concepts properly. What was explained to us in Tibet was only the version of the Chinese government—I did not imagine there was a different world from the one they told us about. Arriving in India had opened the doors of the world for me, and not only those of the Tibetan truth. I began to study the history of all countries, to hear and learn new languages, experience new religions, respect them and decide, with full freedom, what I wanted to be, what sort of man I wanted to be, which way to go in life, and so on.

India has been for me, as for everyone else, what Chinese-occupied Tibet had not been for me for eight years of my life. India is a country of possibilities and choice for us Tibetans, with no one dictating what to do or think.

I was born in Tibet, but I grew up in a new Tibet in Dharamsala, under the blessings of His Holiness the Dalai Lama and the kindness of India and our supporters.

Despite this, when I was 17 years old and had finished school, the desire to find my parents, to bridge the differences that created a wedge between my old world and the new one, was too hard to resist. I decided to go back on the same path I had taken years earlier. I decided to return to Tibet.

It was the end of March and I think I've felt such fear only a few times in my life. On the border, my uncle was waiting for me. We walked many hours through the night, until we reached his house. My parents were there, waiting for me, with eyes filled with tears, watching mine, which were dry.

I stayed for a month, locked up at home. Since I did not speak Chinese, if someone had asked me a question, I would have been finished.

I did not want to stay. It was a prison for me, without any kind of future. It seemed to me that every day my head was ready to explode from the pressure of my thoughts—I would never have a job, a wife, or children if I stayed back, because eventually I would only end up in jail and would never be able to see the light of the sun. The decision was made. With a heavy heart, I decided to return to India. The day came that I knew would be the last in which I saw the faces of the people who gave me birth and raised me. I had to bid them farewell to give myself the opportunity of a new life. I broke my own heart again, conscious that my choice for my future would cost the maternal warmth that I had cried for every night in those nine years away from home.

The return wasn't difficult. I just had to walk without making eye contact and keep my lips sealed.

From my eyes, two tears are falling.

Dadrun,[14] *now I know I made the right decision, even if, at times, I feel like running back to hug them.*

I hope that something will change. I know I am lucky. There are people who cannot come back and others who did not want to go to India, but eventually they are forced to

---

14. The Tibetan name that His Holiness the Dalai Lama gave me— Tenzin (the holder of the teaching) Dadrun (the moonlight to enlightenment).

make this decision only out of fear for themselves and their dear ones' lives. You know that if they didn't do so, their family would end up in laogai.[15] The Chinese did not know of my existence. If they became aware of it and knew that my family sent me to grow under the care of His Holiness, I would have to choose between my future and their lives; I would have to go back to Tibet.

I am really very lucky. I have everything I could have wished for, Dadrun. Although the situation is not good for us Tibetans, at the least I can pray and live freely. Everyday I pray for my family, for the Tibetans and even for the Chinese people!

'What do you want for your country?'

Do you know the popular Middle-Way Approach?

Nodding, I smile at him.

Yes, I would like an outcome that benefits both the Chinese and the Tibetan people. To reach this conclusion required for me a long process and 20 years of following the teachings of His Holiness, but now I know that this is the most desirable solution—that Tibet remains a part of China, with internal autonomy, culture, ethnicity, language and its own freedom.

I am okay to live under China but I want my freedom! I am okay being a citizen of China, but I want to maintain my Tibetan identity. I want Tibet to be able to offer its people what India offered me—a choice.

Hush.

I get lost looking at the expanse of green in front of me. I'm sitting on a plastic rocking chair, with my feet resting on a block of wood that I found outside my room. My thoughts do not stop. It is so hard to write

---

15. *Laogai* are the Chinese concentration camps.

about the pain of a loved one. Earlier, when I felt his life before noting it down, it almost had a different flavour. My view of him does not change, although a bit of sadness enters my heart.

The bell rings at the end of the lesson. I stub out my cigarette—my two children should not see me smoking. I get up, I give him a friendly pat on the back and three kisses to bless him—two on his eyes and one on his forehead.

Dicky

I was sitting on the side of the main street in Suja, looking for a little shelter from the sun. It was too hot that day, and I wanted a sip of water for my dry throat.

Indian heat, even in the foothills of the Himalayas, can be sudden, and it is very good in denying respite. It has no regard for altitude, it is not even concerned that it is the rainy season when water and fresh breeze provide relief. Indian heat stiffens the tonsils and takes away one's energy.

Tsering and I were killing time that monsoon morning, talking and sipping cool drinks in the shelter of a small shack that could be called, with a bit of imagination, a cafeteria. An old lady, driven by the same desire for shade and shelter, was standing a few metres away, staring at us. She just stood there, motionless, gazing at us as if to ask permission to join us for a few minutes at our table—the only one in the area that, apart from being in the shade, also offered a small dusty fan.

Tsering smiled at her and moving a chair, nodded at her to take it.

In my curiosity about fairy tales, myths, and stories, I got lost in the features of this lady. She was old, with a sweet smile and soft contours. Despite the 50 years that separated her from her country of origin, she still wore the traditional Tibetan dress—a grey *chupa*,[16] so in contrast with the brilliant colours of India, and so unsuitable for the hot summer of this subcontinent. About her hips she wore a *pangden*[17] with coloured stripes which in Tibet, the land of snow, means that a woman has been taken in marriage and is no longer free. Even her earrings, blue turquoise supported by a thread of red wool, were from Tibet.

I was not yet confident with the Tibetan language, but I understood from her dark and wrinkled face that she was not moved only by the desire to rest and enjoy the artificial wind from the fan. Her almond-shaped eyes darted from me to Tsering, from him to me and back again, revealing the secret that the real purpose of her visit was to share some thoughts.

World-wide, elders love to tell stories.

Strong in her courage, once she had overcome the first moment of hesitation, she asked us where we came from, what we were doing there, and then, without giving time for answers, she started her story. A short story, really short—the story of her life.

My name is Dicky. I am 87 years old. I was born in Kongpo. It is a very happy place, so much so that many of those like me who have decided to escape to India, have returned after a few months. Kongpo is all green and full of flowers. In the morning, the stream flowing in the direction of the village wakes us up with the sun. It's a happy place. Or it was, 50 years ago.

---

16. The *chupa* is the typical Tibetan dress—long and with a sash which tightens at the hips, it is generally chosen in dark shades.
17. The *pangden* is a Tibetan apron worn by married women to emphasize their marital bond. It is generally brightly striped with bands of colour, in contrast to the plain colours of dark shades of the dress worn beneath.

I made the decision to leave my country after the Chinese occupation and the beginning of the tortures, in 1959. The government in Beijing had just sucked out money and possessions from the aristocracy. The dissolution of the middle class would be next. I was a part of it. In fact, my family were paying taxes with three hundred sacks of flour a year. But we had seen what happened after you delivered everything you had. When there was nothing left, soldiers were not the politest or most well-mannered people—they began beatings, imprisonment, and torture.

Kongpo was a happy place, before 1959.

I remember the escape. I was a part of a group of people who had decided to tackle this trip together. We walked during the night and we spent the day hidden in the forest. We travelled the whole way on foot, sharing and experiencing many problems. I lost my husband during the journey. He was behind us and his whole group ended up in the hands of the Chinese militia. He did not reach prison, they killed him first. I lost many companions in the harsh climate of the Himalayas. Some days it was almost impossible to find water and many ended up dead because they were too weak to go on.

The Indian army received us at the border, due to the request made by His Holiness the Dalai Lama. He had not forgotten us. He didn't, ever. When he arrived in India he requested the authorities to leave the border open—he knew that many of his people would follow him. It is only thanks to the kindness, the care, and the goodness of His Holiness that we did not die of hunger, thirst, and fatigue. He knew that we were not used to the hot weather that reigns here, so he prepared the ground to enable us to acclimatize.

Since I knew how to plant and work the leaves that give us beer, I was assigned to Suja.

Across the road, a woman leaned over a balcony and shouted, 'Dicky, come home! Lunch is ready!'

She smiled at us. She stopped talking. When she was about to go, I took her hand and ask her, 'Are you happy?'

I'm really very happy. The climate here is moderate, there is water, there is His Holiness to bless us, and I can see the mountains. Some are green, some brown, and then there is snow. I've always loved snow, ever since I was a child.

She smiled at me, touched my head to wish me good luck, then she grasped the rosary she had on her left wrist. While reciting the mantra which she only whispered, probably because the practice was considered to be a personal one, she walked home, slowly, step by step, until her long white braid disappeared behind the door of an old building.

I picked up a fresh bottle of cola and leaned back into the little plastic chair I was sitting on. It was a story of only a few minutes, in the slow time and space that only the Himalayan mornings can grant.

It was time for us to go, too, much richer than we were before.

Ven. Bagdro

Two thousand metres above sea level, in a suburb of the Kangra district in the state of Himachal Pradesh, separated from China only by mountain ranges, lies a village known as Little Lhasa. This is in India and, if you are in a taxi, to reach this place you should cross the busy and colourful Indian market of Dharamsala. At the end of this ever-noisy road, you will notice a steep incline, outlining an imaginary line between the liveliness of Indian market and the green silence of the forest. You should drive carefully, with plenty of skill, using the clutch, and in 15 minutes you will start to see houses decorated very differently from the usual Indian houses. There are small monasteries, bookshops, and restaurants that take the visitor to the centre of McLeod Ganj, all with curtains hanging in front of their entrance—generally white, embroidered in blue, red, and green.

Since 1960, this place has been home to His Holiness the Dalai Lama and the Tibetan government-in-exile.

Two main roads meet at a square and create a triangle that is now home to approximately eleven thousand people. Most of them know the monk Venerable Bagdro.

Before I reached this place and learnt to listen to the voices from the road, I had no idea who he was. I was very lucky to immediately get his phone number. I had to wait only a few hours before meeting him—the time he needed to climb the mountain to this small village that was our home. He called me around four o'clock and told me to come to a restaurant just off the main square. I went in to find him surrounded by thousands of small shopping bags. He was dressed in red, with a shaved head, a smile that covered the entire width of his sweet face, and eyes like almonds, stretched horizontally. He decided to sit in the large terrace. There were few clouds that day and the view from the terrace was the perfect sight to calm the spirit—a green valley, decorated by small, coloured roofs and prayer flags fluttering against a blue sky. He ordered black tea for both of us, shook my hands, and asked how he could help me.

After the pleasantries, I smiled. I introduced myself and ask him to tell me his story. He began quietly, letting the tea cool down.

My name is Bagdro. I am 39 years old now—at least that is what my passport says—and I come from Tibet.

More precisely, I was born in 1968—I believe that was the year. I was born into a peasant family consisting of two sisters, a brother, my parents and I, in a small village called Gyepa, near Lhasa, which, at the time, had a population of 250 souls.

The Chinese arrived in Tibet in 1949, talking about liberation. They brought us their weapons and their education. We, however, had no enemies and even though our education was happening within monastic walls, we were a cultured people. We were not interested in physics and chemistry, I admit it, but our culture was no less than the progressive Western one. While humans went to the moon, we explored the inner world and learned to live peacefully.

Now I know—and everyone knows by now—that the Chinese did not come to give us progress. They came only for our land and what it contained. They were not interested in the people who lived there.

The example of this lack of interest in us as human beings was illustrated for me by the life-story of the man who gave me life, my father. In his youth, he was a monk. When the Cultural Revolution began, he was captured, imprisoned, beaten, and forced to marry on pain of death. Poor man, forced to betray his nature in order not to lose his life.

Six thousand monasteries were destroyed, sacred images decapitated, burned, and in their place portraits of great Chinese politicians were placed. All was lost. A whole tradition gone. Who said they wanted to help us?

Sipping his tea, looking straight into my eyes, he smiled and continued:

I spent my childhood totally isolated from everything, in a world that was not Tibet. I remember when, for the first time, I met a blonde girl with blue eyes. I initially thought she came from another planet.

We had no electricity, no internet, no newspapers that could tell us what lay beyond the borders of our land. The elders could not even tell us about our mountains and our history. The only truth that we knew was what we saw with our eyes—what the Chinese wanted us to see. There was no other information.

I decided to become a monk after the death of my elder sister, in November 1985. I was 17 years old. I know now, that before 1949, even though our people were not rich, no one had ever died for lack of food. I must confess that I made this decision to become a monk because I was hungry. Initially it was not due to any calling that led me to wear red clothes and shave my head. I knew that in the monastery I would never suffer the terrible condition of hunger, so I made a deal with my stomach. I had no doubts about the road I was undertaking.

He paused. He was thinking aloud.

Now, whoever dies in prison becomes food for others . . .

By cutting trees and building dams, we will also begin to suffer thirst . . .

I waited a year before receiving permission to become a monk. Permission—and this is freedom?

I used to cook for 250 monks. I would wake up at three in the morning, go into the kitchen, and begin to prepare soup and tea. I liked doing it. It gave me peace to handle vegetables, flour, and milk—the peace that comes when your stomach is full and you can sleep without cramps in the belly. Suffering from hunger is one of the punishments that, once you overcome it, it makes you feel real happiness.

After some time, however, this was not the only reason for my contentment. I began to appreciate the monastery, in all its facets. I found good teachers who, day after day, taught me how to cultivate my inner self. Although I didn't receive Buddhist teachings—there were no lamas in the monastery—prayers and music began to explain my culture to me. I wasn't exposed to a philosophical reflection on my religion as debating was not allowed. Rituals, however, combined with the discipline of practising them, gave rise to a habit in me which explained the rhythms of my people.

In Tibet there is a proverb which says, 'There are three things that cannot be long hidden—the sun, the moon, and the truth.'

Fate wanted to open my eyes and tell me about a reality I didn't know about. One day I came across the book My Land, My People[18] *by His Holiness the Dalai Lama. The author of*

---

18. *My Land, My People* is the autobiography of Tenzin Gyatso, the Fourteenth Dalai Lama of Tibet. Written and published in 1962, it has been translated into many languages and tells the life-story of the spiritual head Tibet.

this autobiography was totally unknown to me—my parents had never told me about him. Inside the monastery, the only pictures that I had been given were those of Mao and Stalin. I didn't know the face of this man, as indeed I barely knew that of Buddha.

It was an unusual story. I wasn't aware of even the basics it talked of. It told me of my people, of our traditions, and whispered to me of the smiling monk on the cover of the book. Before that moment, I had always thought that Dalai Lama was a name used to describe a god far away from this land. I never thought it was a man of flesh and bones, as I was.

I immediately understood why no one had ever spoken to me about this. I understood why so many people had died, why monasteries had almost become prisons. I began to understand the meaning behind the slogan that I had sometimes seen on the walls, walking through the capital—Free Tibet. I understood why a number of my people were exiled.

I also understood what everyone in Tibet was now whispering, 'Our leader is not Mao, but the Dalai Lama.'

I was maybe 18 when that night, after closing the door of my room, I spent all the hours of darkness reading and re-reading that autobiography by the faint light of a candle.

I was completely shocked. I cried. I remember very well the taste of those tears and the anger that gripped my heart. I went home. I cut two gashes in the shape of a cross through two photos of the president of the Communist Party and hung them up upside down. I spent days writing various bills, reciting, 'Free Tibet, let the Dalai Lama come back!' and a letter of request for independence for my country. I hung a pair of the bills in the monastery and one in the

Chinese office in my village. I went to Norbu Ri,[19] where foreigners were taking pictures, I gave one to two Americans.

In September and October of 1987, in the Drepung and Sera monasteries[20] in Lhasa, two of the three largest pro-independence protests that the Land of Snows had ever seen after 1959 were staged. Our beautiful capital turned into a hellish prison that offered three different destinies to anyone who had taken part in the protests—death, torture, or forced labour. In my heart I could not say what was more desirable.

Then, next year, on the 5th of March the third largest protest took place.

It was the time of the festival of prayer, the monlam,[21] and Lhasa was flooded with many Tibetan pilgrims and invaded by four thousand Chinese soldiers, who were not wearing their usual uniform. That day should have marked a moment of connection with the divine, through prayers and good deeds. We were driven by the desire for freedom and our Chinese comrades were disguised as monks in yellow and red robes, and they had orders to kill anyone who protested.

I went to the temple of Jokhang,[22] prayed to Lord Buddha and thought of His Holiness. I drank, ate, and wrote a letter

---

19. Norbu Ri is a hill upon which stands the famous monastery of Lamaling.
20. Dreupung and Sera, along with Gaden, are the names of the three biggest monasteries in Tibet. Only in these monastic schools can monks get a degree in philosophy, starting from simple level to reach the Geshe degree (equivalent to PhD) in Buddhism.
21. *Monlam* is a Tibetan word meaning 'prayer'. All the minor festivals that contain spiritual rituals are also known by this name.
22. The *Jokhang* is the most important Buddhist temple in Lhasa. Built in the seventh century by King Songtsen Gampo, it contains the sacred statues representing Akshobya Vajra (the Buddha at age eight) and Jowo Sakyamuni (the Buddha at age twelve).

to my parents that vaguely followed this track, 'I'm going to Lhasa. I am going to die for our country, for our freedom. Don't cry for me, because many will pray for me and I shall be saved.'

I joined other monks with the same aspirations. We were quite convinced that we could really change something. We believed that our voice would be heard. We thought that by sacrificing our lives, the world would be made aware of what was going on and others after us would have a different life.

It didn't happen like that.

We didn't even manage to start the protest, so important for us. I remember that I had only time to scream, 'Go away! Let the Dalai Lama return!' Then there were just flashes. Tear gas prevented us from seeing what was taking shape around us. The girl who a second before was standing next to me was now lying on the ground with a hole in her heart. Other companions were down too, blood flowing from their heads and legs. I remember an incredible pain. I could not determine if it was caused by the bullet that stuck me in the leg, or by the fact that a children's monastery was being attacked. The children were seven, maximum ten years old, and they were being beaten to death with wooden rods and sticks.

The soldiers were on a killing spree, mercilessly shooting in every direction. They didn't care whether it was children or adults as long as they could shoot the defenceless people who were only raising their voice for freedom. Everything had become a military camp. We wanted to die for our country and it appeared that they were there to grant us that wish.

I just remember these details of 5th March, 1988, although I do not remember where I went after that, or how I got there. I know that I woke up a few days later with the bullet extracted, my wound medicated, and a Tibetan woman taking care of me.

My photo was circulating throughout the city. I spent my days in the mountains and at night I returned to the capital to eat and keep abreast of what was happening.

On the 14th and 15th of April of the same year, three vans full of Chinese soldiers went to my family home. Not finding me, they threatened my father. If he did not hand me over, my family would have to suffer the fate that was meant for me. They were given a week to do so or suffer the consequences of hiding me. As a proof that the threats were real, they shot my dog dead. My father tried to explain to them that my lifestyle was totally different from theirs; he also tried to deny me as a son. He didn't convince them. They went to my old monastery, Gaden. Maybe they would have better luck there, they thought. Their demands were not different, nor were the answers they received and the threats that followed.

When I heard about what had happened, I decided to go home. It was six in the morning on the 17th of April. I cried with my family. At half-past-eight I was arrested.

They took me to the prison called Gutsa, in the eastern area of Lhasa. I remember the phrase that for months I would have to hear all day, 'The world revolves around how China wants it to.' They locked me in handcuffs, which with every movement came increasingly close to slitting my wrists. 'Free Tibet?' they asked, kicking me and beating me with sticks.

I was terrified. Day and night I was exposed to the screams of other inmates, 'Enough, please!' 'Kill me, but just stop it!' was what I said while they kept me hanging upside down without any clothes. It was hell on earth.

The time came to change my manacles—both on my feet and hands, three pounds each. I was not even allowed to sleep to escape the pain—to sleep meant to receive more blows. Days of insomnia followed, with eyelids that no longer listened to my will. I was woken up by fists.

He stops for a moment and sips some more tea.

Then came the interrogation. I remember a small table with assorted contraptions of torture and voices asking always the same thing, 'How much money did you receive from the Dalai Lama for the protests?' 'How many people were you?' 'The names . . .'

My answer was always the same, 'I don't know what you are talking about.' Calling me a liar, they would open my mouth wide to give me electric shocks over and again.

After a long, long time, when I collapsed from the torture, I would be sent back to my cell. The day after I recovered, the procedure was the same, but the places of torture changed. First, they targeted my back, and then my head, my ears, and so on until they had exhausted all orifices my body had to offer. If I didn't faint from the strength of the electrical shocks, I knew I would have been beaten senseless.

The creativity in torture did not end, either. Unlike my memory, it was not limited.

I spent hours without shoes standing on a board covered with nails, to improvise a tightrope. My shoulders were held down, while pieces of glass were pushed into my calves.

I become their ashtray—cigarette burns on my face and my body were perhaps the feeling that I minded the least. I hated being upside down, naked, with tubes in every hole of my body, firing water jets without end.

After ten months of torture, I had problems everywhere in me. And not just physical. In hunger I ate soap, and thirst led me to drink my own urine. When they found me with some bread, given to me by a friend, they stole it and fed me with a soup made of excrement.

But everything has an end, and so for me too the end of that cycle came eventually.

I changed prison. I was moved to Drapche.[23] About this place, I have only fragments of memory of the terror that I was subjected, that occurred every day at 11 in the morning. They took the healthier prisoners and extracted from them a litre of blood to be sold or donated to Chinese hospitals.

He stopped and began again to think out loud.

If we are equal, why do the worst jobs go to Tibetans? If we are equal, why are only Chinese allowed in school? Why?

Then he resumed.

I tried to kill myself several times. I reached a weight of 40kg. Just when death was going to carry me away, after three years of hell, I was released. For them it was better that I die outside the prison walls. Luckily, I survived and am happy to be alive to tell the story to the world.

One night near the end of my captivity, I had a dream. A beautiful Tibetan woman with flowers in her hands served me milk. Offering me a place to sleep, she gave me peace for at least one night. A few months later a tulku[24] explained to me that it was Tara[25] who had helped me regain my strength.

---

23. Drapche, also known as Drapchi Prison, is located a few kilometres north of the Potala Palace in Lhasa. Its official name is Tibetan Autonomous Prison. Built in 1960, it is described in the testimonies of ex-political prisoners as one of the most terrifying prisons.

24. *Tulku*, 'being with extraordinary qualities', is a Dharma teacher of many reincarnations, a Bodhisattva who continues to emerge, driven by love for all sentient creatures, to help everyone to achieve enlightenment.

25. Tara, 'star', known in Tibetan as Jestun Dolma, is a female transcendental Bodhisattva. She represents compassionate activities.

Release from prison, in fact, was much the same as being still there. I felt that there was always someone following me, watching my steps, my actions. Fear immobilized me. I saw freedom before my eyes but I knew that if I reached for it, it would be ripped away from my grasp. I could not go to my old monastery or any other place of worship. I was constantly controlled, permanently trapped by a fear that didn't let me spread my wings.

Then I decided to fly again. But my flight could not take place in those high snow-capped mountains of Tibet. The only way to feel air in my lungs again, in a life that made sense to live, was exile. At that time I was 23 years old.

Some friends gave me some money—a few yuan. I asked my parents to come to Lhasa and we went to a restaurant. They ate, but I did not touch the food. I knew it would be the last time that I met them. I told them that I would be gone a few months to visit a monastery away from home. I lied. I could not tell them the truth—they would have been in danger again.

On that July night, I began the long journey to the Nepalese border. There were seven of us, and I was very sick. We walked for three months on snowy roads littered with corpses and skeletons. I thought the same fate would also befall us. I was wrong. I arrived in Nepal, where I was hospitalized. I remained for a month under the care of a Tibetan hospital that hid me from the outside. There were too many Chinese spies and they could not let them find me just when I was almost safe. After some time, I started my journey again.

And there it was, at last—India. It was September 1991.

One morning, many days later, the air began to have a different thickness. Although I didn't realize it at that time, that was the morning I truly began to feel alive again. A man close to His Holiness came to get me and said that I had a special audience with the Dalai Lama. I can't describe the feeling I experienced. Maybe I should just say that it was happiness, the happiness that I had experienced earlier only a few times in my life. It was like a dream, but mixed with the reality of life, with a sick body and a spirit ready to heal.

I spent more than an hour in a personal audience with His Holiness, which changed the motives that were driving me till then. I must admit that for months before this audience, I was caught up by an ignoble desire. I wanted to return to Tibet and kill. To kill and give pain, as I had received, to the Chinese. During the audience, His Holiness spoke to me in a calm voice about another approach to resolve the Tibetan issue, a more effective way. He saw a way that would be of benefit to both sides—for us and for China. It was the way of non-violence.

A sentence at that time got deeply imprinted in my heart. His Holiness said, 'Violence creates more violence.'

He encouraged me to write, to cure my heart by putting on paper the pain that I carried within, and thereby to free myself from it. The welfare process began that day when he brushed my face and, as if by magic, the air began to weigh less.

On that day, many things began to take a different form. The dream took shape, which helped me get out of my prison.

First, a French lady hosted me for a year in France in a centre for people with psychological problems. Then in 2001 I spoke at the British Parliament. In 2003, I spoke at the European Parliament in Belgium. My voice did not have great resonance and certainly did not change the fate of my country. In 2008 there were more protests in Tibet—two thousand people died and another thousand were reported missing.

In that year, I went to the Spanish court, where I met representatives of the Peoples Republic of China. They called me 'The Dalai Lama's dog' and they painted me as a very dangerous man.

He laughed.

Dangerous? I'm not dangerous. Thirty people sacrificed themselves in November in Tibet but not because of me or because of His Holiness. The monasteries are jails and prisons are concentration camps. It's obvious that people choose death as a form of protest!

I, we, His Holiness, we all want peace.

Why does the EU not do anything? They say they are against anything that revisits the Nazi period but, though no one wants to speak about it, now, even in 2012, there are dozens of labour camps in Tibet.

If there is no change, there will be no future.

Today, the only hope that I carry in my heart is that more people reach India safe and sound. It's only a hope, a desire that does not take into account the welfare of Tibet as a nation but only the love for my people who are not free in their own land. However, if Tibetans continue to leave the Land of Snow, Tibet will only become purely Chinese, and will become less relevant to the Tibetans, its true owners.

This hope, however, is unrealistic. The borders are closed. They are dangerous, and to cross them means risking life — not only due to the difficult environmental conditions on the way, but also due to the risk of being shot at sight by the Chinese soldiers who guard the borders. To go legally through that invisible line is out of the question. Tibet's doors are closed to the Tibetans living outside Tibet, sometimes even to people who come from Europe and the United States.

He paused and smiled at me.

The tea was cold now, an hour had just passed. I could not drink it. I noted down every word that he spoke. On the horizon, the sky took new shades. I believed that the sun would bless us only a few moments more—the monsoon was taking over. I had always wondered how the temperature in the Himalayas was able to fall so quickly.

'What would you like for Tibet?' I asked.

I am a simple monk, too ignorant to be able to give an answer that takes into account not just my selfishness and my ego, but that which addresses a bigger plan. In my heart I want my people to be free and independent, as we were once. I know what I want will probably not happen—China is too powerful.

However, I hope that a day will come when we would have an autonomy under China, with control of our internal matters as enshrined in China's constitution. I also wish that more Tibetans—young and old—will be able to reach this place and hear, if only once, the voice and message of His Holiness.

I hope that no one, due to fear, will be silenced and not tell the true story of Tibet to their newborns, because silence is death.

'How did you get over your past?'

Answering this question is always very complicated. To explain beliefs of the heart is always more difficult than answering through reason and scientific logic. If I had to give an answer, avoiding logic, I would say that my strength is derived from the constant teachings of the Dalai Lama.

To be honest, it was that morning, when the air inexplicably became lighter, after meeting my true leader, the reincarnated Buddha, His Holiness the 14th Dalai Lama.

That day something really changed in me. It was like having a long broken spring readjusted and functioning again, all by itself, magically. Since then, slowly, everything has fallen into place.

After all, all living beings suffer. Sometimes you only need to understand that, with exercise, we can control the anger we have inside, the pain that surrounds us. It is not an easy route, nor a short one. In the beginning, when I heard sirens, fear overtook me again and some nights were filled with nightmares. Now, I do not suffer anymore. I remember, but the past does not overshadow my present.

I cannot claim to have reached this state of being with my own strength. I think the compassionate care of His Holiness was an ointment that gave birth to the healing process. Some people describe him as a being with human features but with supernatural qualities. Some say he eats, sleeps, breathes as each of us, just to maintain a semblance of normality; for some, he has already attained Buddhahood and is back among us just to help us to do the same, moved by compassion and love. For my part, I can say that even if he is just another human, he is the most special one of all living beings.

Then, to help me, I had prayers, meditation, walks, and even writing. To write of my injuries and my past has helped me to get past them and allowed me to leave the prison that did not allow me to live.

'Don't you feel anger towards the Chinese people?'

How can I? Not all Chinese agree with the government that commands them. Many of them suffer the same fate as I did. Many also support us. As for my tormentors, they do their job; if they refuse they become victims themselves. Each of them has a family and I know how important our loved ones are for us. I know what it means to be hungry and to need money and food. They too are human beings as we are. Anger destroys us. We should just let negative emotions go and focus on positive things instead. If I was angry, I wouldn't receive invitations from so many countries around the world asking me to speak. I would not have the strength, nor the support, to change, or at least to try to change something.

You must give up some emotions but remember others. If you hold the Buddhist teachings in your heart, they will help you to have a true view of reality that manifests itself within and outside. If a stranger reports a negative feeling inside me due to my misbehaviour, most likely at the same time I'm giving birth to a negative karma. It is a two-way road that elapses between two different entities—a path of two lanes, with opposite directions but the same intensity.

Raindrops began to fall. The sun was still radiating its light but it would soon be swallowed by the clouds, to appear but once again.

I had no further questions for him. My heart was heavy. Yes, I wanted to take his picture. He pointed me to a place in the open, struck a pose like an ordinary person whose only desire was to have a good shot that portrays him well. He tried various poses. He laughed. He thought he might look younger with another angle of the light. He laughed, and laughed again. I forgot for a moment the pain I was feeling in the wake of his story and, looking at the scars still visible on his face after twenty years, I smiled with the joy this man was giving me.

Before leaving, our tea now stone cold, he shared with me another little secret.

In Tibet we believe in spirits. We believe in energy, and we believe that some dreams reveal fragments of truth. The latest nightmare I've had has been a premonition to me. I dreamed it was 4th March, 2008. I was in Lhasa and a large protest for human rights in Tibet was taking place. Many people were killed.

The next morning I woke up sweating and, thinking it was a memory of the past that came again that night, I washed my face. I did not give importance to it. I went out and met a friend to spend some time together.

At one o'clock of the same day, what I had seen in the night happened.

He laughed.

You asked me what I hoped. In truth, for now, I just hope that these dreams will not occur again. If they do, I hope that they are just dreams. If they must show me the future, I hope they will show me a day in which I will walk the streets of my city and the Dalai Lama will bless us all from the Potala.[26]

That day, it was he who was blessing me, saying a mantra over the rosary I wore on my wrist, before saying goodbye.

---

26. The Potala Palace is located in Lhasa on Mount Marporì. It is considered to be the abode of Avalokitesvara, the Buddha of compassion. Until 1959, it was the main residence of the Dalai Lama.

Renewal

10th August, 2017

Three years have passed since fate snatched me from those beautiful Indian mountains. It is 10th August, 2017, and, equipped with a small suitcase, after a month in which I took in my hands the thesis that came to life exactly five years ago, I go to Kashmere Gate to catch a bus to Dharamsala. Delhi traffic has almost made me miss my bus. Perhaps it would have been better to miss it—luck hasn't allowed me to choose between a Volvo and a public bus. My bus has no air conditioning. Seats can be reclined a little and smell of papier-mâché. Twelve hours of travel in those conditions makes me now feel like I must take a few moments to describe my feelings.

Delhi during this time of the year seems more chaotic than usual. Rain slows the traffic and humidity settles on your skin, making it heavy. Imagine wearing hiking boots and a sweatshirt, and finding yourself forced into a long metallic box with 50 other people, without air, in the middle of the city, in temperatures of 40 degrees, with two hundred per cent humidity in the air.

The first six hours of my bus journey passed like this. Later, at night, on the highway and then among the first hills, it became more pleasant.

We are in the middle of the monsoon season and, with my back aching, McLeod Ganj welcoms me with floods and a fog.

To be honest, I'm happy. I've always liked the monsoon. Strange as it may seem, I've always liked rain and humidity. Not that I like the feeling of a damp bed or permanently damp hair. And I am not a fan of a sore throat and the cough that follows. But the mountains in the monsoon, in the hours of peace, paint so clearly the idea that everything has an end—a respite, even in the most ardent storm, is required.

So here I am back again, to give myself some respite after a period of life that I would call a storm. During the last year, I lost my stability centres. I lost them through being in love with a man for whom I gave up who I was and where I came from. Now that life has forced me to find myself, I give myself a respite, starting from where I left being who I was.

So here I am, doing what I loved the most when I was 22, and I find myself still in love with it at 27, sitting down to breakfast in the space outside a small street café, amid the sounds of eight o'clock in the morning, when only women and elderly men, walking in the direction of the temple, break the tranquillity of nature with whispered prayers pronounced on rosaries of one hundred and eight beads, sliding quickly between the fingers of their left hands.

I loved to write in this place. I still love it.

The coffee is as poor as it was years ago. The fog wets my face, just like it did years ago. Some places change more slowly, or not at all, even when your life has changed so much from earlier.

Let's step back a little.

I reached Dharamsala yesterday morning. The faces I met were old faces who had been my family for many years. There were also many new ones.

Yesterday, after the 12-hour bus journey into these hills, my tiredness led me to take a taxi to Suja. There lies the school that is home to the two children who are a huge part of my heart. They are two kids who were, at the time I first met them, four and six years old. Now they are big, almost taller than me. They will soon enter the teenage years. It is the second Saturday of the month and, like every Saturday like this (save in winter, when they have stayed with me in Delhi for the last five years) it brings me back to McLeod Ganj to be with them. It is the first time, however, that we come back to a hotel and not to a home. A few months ago, thinking that my life is no longer here, I decided to let go of the four walls that gave me the illusion that, if I wanted, I could come back. After all, this place will always be home, even though I do not have a shelter made of bricks to sleep in.

It is also the first time, after months in which I repeated these gestures without actually being present with my thoughts, I choose and I want to be here. The period in which discomfort did not allow me to be mentally present is coming to an end. I was always held back by the lack of him, him whom I missed, not realizing that I was losing myself to an equally lost soul. I really thought that I had found my way, I thought it worthwhile to leave everything, forgetting the lessons that this community had repeated to me for years. I really thought that my happiness came from outside. Now that I am recovering my balance, I understand better that harmony comes only from within.

Yesterday was spent travelling between mountains, memories, and fatigue. I had dinner with these two children who have become part of my everyday life and my thoughts. And I had a soft bed to rest in.

Today I really return to the life that Delhi took me away from.

The alarm rings at six. The children are sleeping. I, however, get dressed and start to climb the mountains. I stop for a light breakfast with some friends, then walk up the mountains in the company of a lady who has been my elder sister and who is with me today to help with translation. Thirty minutes walking uphill brings us to a small house, consisting of one tiny room, in the middle of nowhere. If you do not know where to look, the untrained eye won't spot it. A woman, two monks, and a *ngapa*[27] are present. We are here for a prediction.

If the Western world has forgotten the non-scientific nature of certain rituals, these people have preserved them as a precious treasure. I find myself to be a hybrid of two beliefs—I think that, though not real, the sacredness of certain gestures is an experience not to be missed. It gives you strength, courage, and hope.

We sit on the floor in front of the bed where an old man sits cross-legged. Like all of his kind, he has long thin hair, tied in a ponytail.

We're here because I need to find myself and because now, after so many months of loss, I want to

---

27. *Ngapa* is the name by which the tantric practitioners are known. Generally, they differ from monks since they can have relationships with women and get married. As for their physical aspect, though dressed in the red robes typical of the monastery, to differentiate themselves they often have long hair, not shaved, tied in a ponytail.

live again. The old man produces some rectangular sheets and some dice. He prays. I ask a question and he, murmuring mantras and blowing on the dice in his hands, has just seen a number. Guru Rinpoche[28] looks at us from the eyes of a lofty of a statue. He scrutinizes us from the *thangka*[29] that depicts him.

The man opens the *pecha*.[30] He reads and writes down a prayer that will be performed to remove obstacles.

He throws the dice.

I am amazed at the responses of different people, after many months, as they always match one another. I lost something along the way over the years and this led me to feel perdition and pain. I lost God, my god, and the only way to rebuild *me* is to find *him*.

I know where he lives. I'm sitting in the cafeteria in front of his home. I kill the time while I pluck up courage, writing and watching the people who walk up and down this street. It's always scary to return home when you've been away for so long. It's always scary to feel good when you have been lulled so long in malaise.

My God still resides here. Our connection has never faded and when my world turned dark and black,

---

28. Guru Rinpoche, known as Padmasambava in Sanskrit, was a great Indian master who went to Tibet in the eighth century and, according to tradition, drove out demons and opponents of the Dharma, as well as helping with the construction of the Potala Palace. He gave many teachings in Tibet. He is considered to be a Bodhisattva.
29. A *thangka*, variously spelled *tangka*, *thanka*, or *tanka*, is a Tibetan Buddhist art form, painted on canvas or executed as silk appliqué, usually depicting a Buddhist deity, scenes, or a mandala. Thangka serve as an important teaching tool, depicting the life of the Buddha, various influential lamas, and other deities and Bodhisattvas.
30. *Pecha* (Tibetan: དཔེ་ཆ་) is a Tibetan word meaning 'book', but in particular it refers to the traditional Tibetan loose-leaf books related to Buddhism.

when I did not want to consider him, when I ignored him, he sent me sparks of light that have brought me back here, in front of his house.

What I will do is pay the bill. Entering his house, I will prostrate. I will be intoxicated with the smell of incense in this house. I will change the language in which I think, switch to Tibetan, and I will try to find him inside me.

It's a long time since I have worn the red blessed string on my left arm. It's a long time since I took *mani rilbu*,[31] the three blessed pills, upon waking up in the morning. It's been too long since I offered alms to the poor.

Today, I'll fix all this while I am trying to change myself back again. Because, while everything changes and nothing stays the same, the Tibetan community changes too slowly for anyone to be able to observe it. So, in the storm of the change that shocked me, I find, resting on a rock, that no matter how much the wind howls and the waves beat mercilessly, I remain stable, firm.

Because though everything changes, the essence of Tibet survives.

---

31. *Mani rilbu* are compound pills made from special ingredients, given by the Dalai Lama Trust, which is located at Namgyal Monastery, Tsuglagkhang. They are blessed seeds on which special prayers have been made for months. It is advised to eat three of them every morning, after washing one's face (symbolically representative of the body) and cleaning one's room (symbolically representative of the mind).

Gu-Chu-Sum

The monsoon is late. I take this opportunity to wear light clothes that cover my body. The sun and the air are as warm as if they were coming out of an oven that has just finished working after hours and hours. I breakfast on my usual unsweetened tea, a piece of white bread, and eggs.

Breakfast for an Italian overseas, especially when one does not have one's own kitchen, is always complicated. Mocha coffee is a dream, not to mention espresso. Bread with Nutella is a distant memory, and croissants are like a vision of another world.

To accept different habits always takes time.

I wait for Tsering's arrival. His room is located a few kilometres from here. He doesn't usually use taxis, so I'll have to arm myself with patience and wait for him to walk up to me.

While waiting, I get lost in the thoughts of how difficult it is to learn ways of life that differ from your own. Few know how it feels to try to fit into a place that is not your own, lined with different shapes and colours. I think of how hard it is to adapt to living in different cultures and traditions, not making too much noise, trying not to be intrusive as a guest in a land that is not your own. And all of this while being driven by a desire to thrive somehow.

Even after two months, I have not yet become accustomed to a simple breakfast.

Today is the first day of many in which we will spend the daylight hours in the compound of the Gu-Chu-Sum movement.[32] Here, we will find and we will talk to refugees who arrived in India after years of torture and imprisonment in Tibet.

Right now I am not aware of that which, within a few hours, I will come to understand. While I sip the mud-water that they sell as coffee, I am not yet aware of some basic truths about this subcontinent.

It took me years to connect the dots that I collected during my stay in India. With hindsight, many years later, I start to have an idea of what happened that day, during my visit to Gu-Chu-Sum.

Six years have passed since that morning, and it took me six years to conceptualize the idea of the existence of vibrations. The constant presence of energy that can, if intense, be perceived in the air—sometimes strong enough to create a reaction in the body and mind.

I will explain what happened that morning in July 2012.

The Gu-Chu-Sum association is not far from my house. We go via alleyways, so narrow that we have to walk sideways between the houses, which will take us directly there. There are very narrow steps, and some flat roofs to cross, and then we find ourselves on the main road. If we had walked the conventional way, it would have taken 20 minutes. This improvised walk saves us half the time, though I, with my Italian legs, risked a broken arm or leg a dozen times.

---

32. *Gu-Chu-Sum* literally means 'nine, ten, three'. It is the name of the association that brings together former prisoners of *laogai* (Chinese concentration camps). It is located in Dharamsala on Jogivara road.

65 • GU-CHU-SUM

The Gu-Chu-Sum building is just like thousands of others from the outside. It is only a small building with a shop at the base selling Tibetan handicrafts and a Japanese restaurant. But the energy that you feel when you are inside the building is completely different. I had never experienced such a change in my sense of well-being, so suddenly and so hard, in my entire life. One minute we were laughing at my lack of ability to walk and now we're both dumbstruck at the entrance, with no capacity for movement or speech. Only our eyes carry on, gazing at the pictures hanging on the yellowed walls—photos never seen, witnesses that I won't photograph. There are things that should remain where they are and must be spoken only in that place—at least, this is my excuse for not having the courage to frame tortured women, lifeless faces covered in blood, images full of such shocking pain.

We take a few steps forward, but the air is really heavy. It seems that the atmosphere weighs like a rock on our heads. Finally we come to the first floor where there is an office. I slink inside. The energy of this place is waiting at the door and cannot enter.

Eight eyes stop working and look at us, waiting to know what we want and who we are. Tsering comes forward and starts to introduce us, 'My sister and I were wondering if it would be possible to talk to the refugees staying in this compound. She's doing research for a thesis on the testimonies of people who have decided to leave Tibet.'

The man at the desk smiles at me, and then scowls at my friend with his almond-shaped eyes. It is easy to understand what he is asking right now, and his response confirms my assumption. 'I am just here to help with people who only speak their local dialects.'

The man stands up. He has a heavy voice and rough movements. Words come from his mouth, and I do not understand what he's saying. Tsering is like a violin string, so I cannot even ask him what the final decree is.

We remain a few minutes at attention, waiting for an answer. Eventually, a smiling man comes towards us. His voice is calm and slow, his movements gentle, 'Follow me. I am very pleased to tell someone my story.'

He knows only a few words of English and my Tibetan is too poor to understand all the nuances that are waiting for me in his story.

We leave the office and continue to the second floor, thrown back into the atmosphere and the feeling that confronted me a few minutes earlier. It's not exactly what I want most in the world. I breathe. Stepping to the door of that office requires the same courage you would need to take a plunge into cold water in the winter.

On every wall hang photos that make me lower my gaze to the floor. I am not ready to face this. I was not prepared for this place. I walk and I follow the man who makes way for me. He stops in front of a locked door. He pulls out a key and opens it, enters the room, and arranges three chairs near the window, giving us a glimmer of light. There is no electricity today.

The walls are full of pictures. We can see just a glimpse of the white colour of the wall—there are so many pictures. It is a rectangular room, and at one end stands a big altar full of flowers offered to Buddha, to the Dalai Lama, and to the Karmapa.[33]

---

33. *Karmapa* or *Gyalpa Karmapa*, literally 'one who performs the Buddhist action', is the head of the Karma Kagyu, the pre-eminent lineage of the Kagyu school, one of the four main schools of Tibetan Buddhism.

We settle down in our chairs. Silence surrounds us. The kind man is waiting for my questions, but my mind is not ready to become stable in this situation. The courage to take a dip into the sea in spring requires energy. To jump into the water in winter, though, requires a bit of madness.

I need a hand to make that dive. He gives it to me, interrupting the silence and beginning to speak about the association which hosts us.

Gu-Chu-Sum of Tibet—we are born from a group of political prisoners who, after the concentration camps, have chosen exile. Courage, strength, and the spirit not to give up, are vital even when all seems impossible.

The movement began on 27th September, 1991 in Dharamsala, India. The organization was registered with the Indian Government on 19th May, 1997. Gu-Chu-Sum of Tibet *is the full name, without abbreviation.*

We wanted to highlight Tibet's name, to indicate all the provinces, religions, gradients, without differentiation, which can be found in this territory. The words gu, chu, *and* sum *are the translation of Tibetan numbers. They mean nine, ten, and three. Nine refers to 27th September, 1987, ten for 1st October of the same year, and three for 5th March, 1988. Only three numbers to remember. These three numbers tell us amazing stories of suffering, determination, and courage. On these dates, Lhasa witnessed three of the major protests that have taken place on Tibetan soil.*

This should not to be taken to mean that our association is made only of memory and is confined to these events. These dates are the symbols that encompass something much bigger—our objective is to remember all circumstances that are linked to the feeling of pain, resentment, and patriotism that exploded in those particular months.

These three dates symbolize what Tibetan people oppose — suffering due to torture, deprivation of freedom, and absence of basic human rights.

These are three dates to remember, three dates to honour those who didn't make it, three numbers to remind us why we are in India.

Our goal is to try to tell the world, through the testimony of the hundreds of people who come to us, about the way Tibetan people are treated by the Chinese government.

Our hope is that China will start to respect human rights and UN standards, and that the world will help us to find a peaceful solution to a real problem that we have been living with for about 60 years now.

Phuntsok Wangdu

The words that he speaks are like the leaves of autumn, massed above one another at the edges of the streets. I am not really able to see them falling; I almost don't even hear their sound, like they are a part of the normality which doesn't attract attention.

I have my gaze concentrated on the face in the picture hanging on the wall behind him. It's a boy, lying naked on the ground. He would be almost my age, certainly in his early twenties. He is devoid of life. Blood was not running through his veins when that picture was taken. It was drying up in his body. His mouth is wide open, like his arms and his legs. His face is resting on the ground.

The speaker watches me stare, and his gaze brings me back to the hour and place which carries my body. I take a deep breath. I realize that three minutes have passed from the time his introduction was concluded, three minutes in which silence has reigned supreme. I notice that his offer of a hand to dispel the discomfort now requires my response.

My thoughts travel from portrait to portrait. I stop myself. I give a wan smile, forced and almost uneasy. With my teeth clenched, I find the courage to form a sentence in a language that is not mine. I ask him to speak freely of his story; the questions will come later.

He speaks Tibetan mixed with the dialect of his region. I must wait for the translation to be able to understand his memories. This time I don't use my pen. My hand is too tired, like the rest of my body. The usual enthusiasm and the energy that, before today, have characterized this journey have almost disappeared. I will let the recorder do the work this time.

I will seek to follow the course of this story while I try to test my comprehension of Tibetan, a perfect excuse to distract myself from the particulars for which I'm not yet prepared.

My name is Phuntsok Wangdu. I was born in 1974, in village Mangchug, in Kham[34] province of eastern Tibet.

Tibet is a place of such beauty that it is difficult to portray it even in a million paintings, especially the remote regions of the country, like where I come from. It is a place of wild expanses that fill themselves with flowers and greenery in some months and in others colour themselves with hues of brown and white, the freshness of the rivers, the culture of a population which no book can contain, especially the myths and especially the philosophy which we are made of.

From my 8th to 16th year, I worked in the countryside. My studies took place at the monastery of Sangag Thekchen Ling,[35] one of the few places where we could still have

---

34. Tibet is composed of three provinces—Ütsang, Kham, and Amdo. Ütsang is situated in the centre, Kham is to the south-east, and Amdo is to the north-east.

35. Sangag Thekchen Ling is the name of a secondary monastery in the region of Kham.

notions, more or less complete, of what should be religion, if we excluded the debates.³⁶ Those weren't permitted.

I also received education for three years at the monastery of Jampaling³⁷ in Chamdo.³⁸ The fortune of youth kissed me, permitting me to be exposed to the truths that few in that period of the history of my country were privy to. In that place, I had an exceptional master—a very important and very qualified monk who, full of courage, was never afraid to expose us to the true philosophy, even though it was prohibited by the new government.

Thanks to his loyalty to the truth, he never allowed us to lurk in the darkness of ignorance. Although we were not allowed officially to keep photos of the Dalai Lama with us, we all knew his face and kept his pictures secretly.

If we add then the fact that sometimes Chinese politics is counterproductive to the aims of the republic, perhaps you can grasp how much I knew of my roots. I remember a public examination that I took part in. One of the questions was: 'Is the current Dalai Lama a negative figure or is the President of the Chinese Republic a negative figure?' They

---

36. Philosophical debate is considered a very important part of the studies of a Tibetan Buddhist monk. It deepens understanding and sharpens the mind, helping the development of wisdom, both conventional and ultimate, which we need for the attainment of Buddhahood. Debating philosophical topics is in accordance with the teachings of the Buddha, who said we should analyse the teachings before accepting them, just like we would analyse the purity and quality of gold before buying it. It is a sequence of questions and answers, based on logical reasoning, put forward in a ritual way. Debates develop between monks who are gesticulating wildly, jumping up and down, and even tossing each other around. The sound of clapping and excited voices is heard while debating.
37. Jampaling is the name of another secondary monastery in the region of Kham.
38. Chamdo is a city situated near the region of Kham.

really believed introducing His Holiness as a negative figure from childhood would do good and build our faith in them.

However, this always worked against them. Indirectly, they created knowledge in us. In the schools it was taught that the negative figure was certainly the opposite of the great Chinese President, that the figure that connotes unpleasantness was that of the Tibetan leader in exile. However, at home, when children asked questions from their parents—Tibetans and non-Chinese, who could recollect the vivid memory of their exposure to reality—they would discover that this person called Dalai Lama who lives in India is actually leading his cause through non-violence.

It was during this period of my life that I began to attend a youth group made up of young people who, with posters and flyers, silently demanded independence for Tibet.

In Tibet, as in the rest of the world, there are different types of people—some who, due to fear, do not speak up and try to keep abreast of things silently, and others who actually involve themselves and publicly give voice to their feelings. I was part of the second group. I was, obviously, arrested by the Chinese. The torture, the imprisonment, and the beatings did not frighten me to stop fighting. On the contrary, they encouraged me to do the exact opposite—they made me want, more deeply, freedom, not only for myself but also for my brothers. If they had not inflicted pain on us, we would have probably understood that we were fighting for nothing. But due to their tortures, our ideas of inequality and lack of freedom were confirmed. Our ideas were even more clear, more real, and gave us the push to believe, more firmly, that truth was on our side.

It is difficult to imagine, but there has been a stark change in my beliefs since then. Now, I am satisfied with autonomy for my country. Back then, I wanted complete independence.

It was 24th of March. It was 28th of April. On those two days I decided to join the efforts that called for freedom through printed flyers that had the slogan 'Bögyalo'— Victory for Tibet! It was not a real protest for we only hung posters in public places and did little else.

In the eyes of Beijing, we committed a big crime. We were considered manipulators of minds. On 2nd May I was arrested by the Chamdo police, beaten, and tortured. It was an interrogation made of beatings. Chinese prisons do not follow the rules of prisons like the rest of the world. I did not have any defence or a lawyer. I was only subjected to the beatings every day for two months. The main questions were: 'Who is behind you? Who is behind all these plots? Who told you to do all of this?' For them, it was difficult to fathom that we could yearn for independence by ourselves even though we were born and raised under Chinese domination. They were convinced that there was a person with a lot of power, living abroad, who was manoeuvring everything from his seat in exile. They were sure that the Dalai Lama paid us to go down the street and 'create havoc' among the population.

What they thought, however, was not true at all.

Everything we did, we thought by ourselves. Our wishes were born within us, without outside influence. In Tibet, it was not difficult to understand the inequality between us and the young men born to Chinese mothers. It was easy to observe the lack of freedom that forced us to disavow essential elements of our beliefs. It was visible to anyone that the Chinese influence was slowly leading to the extinction of our identity, language, customs, costumes, and so on..

No one had influenced me. And I can start to list examples, clear and obvious to anyone. Take for instance the killing of animals in very large numbers, whose meat would be used to feed people of the 'mother republic', deforestation, import of more and more Chinese people onto Tibetan soil, razing of entire Tibetan neighbourhoods, favouring of a new republican style of architecture, and construction of hundreds of dams with the consequent sudden change of habitat that took away our vital resources such as water. All these clearly show that we Tibetans are exploited and suppressed in our own land.

When I was ten years old, all around my village there was the most pristine nature to enjoy freely. I could drink from the stream. I remember the freshness and peace that existed there. But by the time I was 15, everything had changed. With my own eyes I saw that the red flag was destroying the roof of the world.

For those who know what happens to people who try to preserve their beliefs, just one more small pain is enough to blow up all the accumulated rage in your body. I knew the risks I was taking. I saw many of my friends disappear inside the prison. Others, leaving the police station, were covered in blood. But I really believed in what I was doing. It was the same for all prisoners.

In the prison, the methods used were the same for everyone, as was the aim — to change the mentality of the prisoners and, if necessary, use any method including beating, electrocution, and brainwashing with the continuous teachings of Mao and Communism. Until the belief that China and its regime were great was embedded in our minds and in our hearts, they would do everything possible. If it appeared that there was no chance with the person, he would be put to absolute silence.

For me, this belief in China is not possible; for us, it is not right.

The same year, on 2nd July, I was labelled by the Supreme Court as a revolutionary. I was given a sentence of five years *in prison and a suspension for three years of all my political and human rights.*

From that time, I remember two events. From 1st to 4th May, 1998, the prison authorities organized ceremonies that provided for the flag-raising of the red flag, with songs and hymns in honour of the nation. All the six hundred prisoners, including the one hundred and eighty political prisoners, were forced to participate. On one of those occasions, a mass protest interrupted the ceremony. This protest was led by Karma Dawa and Karma Sonam.[39] It was immediately silenced with blood. I remember three young men in their twenties—monks, one of whom had entreated the guards a few hours earlier not to beat an old man but rather to beat him instead, who lost their lives along with seven sisters that day.

In September, two other men, who in the following months did not receive appropriate treatment, followed the same fate.

The other stark memory that I carry with me is the great hope I had in my heart—to die. This was accompanied by the feeling of sadness upon waking every morning when I realized that my dream had not yet come true. Every day was always worse than the previous one. They destroyed my body, hour after hour, almost to the point of making it unusable. Today, years later, I am still under the care of a doctor. I live in India, well fed, but the signs are still clear and the disease is still present.

He falls silent, stands up, and takes off the shirt he is wearing.

I do not understand what he hopes my imagination will come to touch. I see only white bandages that run around the entire circumference of his chest. He senses

---

39. Karma Dawa and Karma Sonam are the names of people—here indicating two individuals.

my confusion at that act and so begins to unroll the three layers of cotton that cover his abdomen. The movements are slow and very delicate. I have time to wonder what he is hiding under so much protection whilst the air becomes warm—it is nearing almost 40 degrees.

I can barely look at the living skin and uncured sores which resemble red meat. I want to close my eyes, but they do not respond to my command. They roam furiously between the photos that surround us and that smiling man who is covering himself now.

I try to control myself as I sip some fresh water. It has no effect. My head hurts and everything seems to spin. Breathe. I just think of the fact that I want to keep the man smiling and if I show all the distress that is devouring me, I know that I will only cause him sadness. Difficult as it is, I begin to understand that for these people, my tears are more painful than their memories and the wounds that will accompany them for the rest of their lives.

Breathe in and breathe out. Again. Repeat. I look for my strength and, remaining silent, without any muscular movement, I make a sign with a twitch of my lips. I'm ready to continue. He resumes.

Another sign that they left with me as an indelible mark for the rest of my life, was to take away from me the ability to memorize. And you can tell from my English! I go to class every day to learn this language and the feeling when I take notes is always that of having learnt something new. The next morning, however, I realize that I do not remember anything.

This fate is not only mine. All my classmates and prisoners live with the same condition. The doctor explained to us that the long exposure to electric shocks and psychological pressures causes these memory holes.

This is my assumption but I believe that, as it happens with trauma, my mind has become accustomed to not absorbing everyday events. It often happens that the memory of pain, with the passage of time, is diluted. I wonder if my brain, in the habit of erasing negative experiences, now does so automatically, even for lessons and positive events. Does it do it as a habit, without being able to discern what is worth remembering and what would cause pain if remembered?

These are just conjectures, suppositions. It is not clear, but we, the ex-political prisoners, are unable to memorize.

In any case, I think I'm lucky when compared to some of my friends. Many are still mentally unstable, years later, and others forget not only their lessons but the faces of their loved ones, or the whole existence of the previous day.

Sometimes it happens that such calm voices, even when they speak of horror, give peace to listening ears. I, in my turmoil this morning, focus on the sound and the tone of this man's voice. I find the stability and strength not to leave this conversation a monologue but, by adding my own voice, make it a dialogue.

'What did you feel, after five years in prison, the day your sentence ended?' I ask.

It was 1st May, 2001. On the first day, I thought it was just a dream. I did not believe I was seeing and experiencing the real world. I had spent five years in prison, including four in isolation. I did not remember what it meant to live among so many people, surrounded by clothes of different colours, animals, roads, and cars. I felt totally confused, stunned. This condition persisted for days, weeks.

They gave me permission to stay in Lhasa for only 20 days. After that, I had to go back home. So I did.

When I arrived, I was not the only one in a state of confusion and surprise. I was standing a few feet away from the white brick house in which I had grown up, unable to move forward. Glued to the ground that should have given me confidence but which now, however, only made my legs shake. My parents looked at me from the window. Even for them it was like being blocked by an invisible wall that did not allow them to move in my direction, which did not really allow them to understand who I was.

They did not hug me and I did not hug them when we faced each other. The silence was interrupted only by the voice, still full of hope, of my mother who whispered, 'Are you really my son?'

How could I blame them? How could I blame myself?

The torture had changed my physical appearance and my psychological attitudes. Not only was it difficult for me to settle for freedom, but even my own parents struggled to see me as their first child.

It is said that, for ordinary beings like us, only time heals such wounds. It was, in fact, the time to recover my instinct for life. As the desire to tell my story to the rest of the world became stronger with every passing day, I could not stay in Tibet.

Forced to stay at home, in the confines of my village, free only with great restrictions and surveillance, I could not remain there. I had to report to the police station every week. If I had refused, my fate would have been life imprisonment. My freedom was actually another form of imprisonment. Unable to re-integrate, because I was unable to forget, it was just as the Chinese government had planned.

I was not free. I could not live a free man, but at the same time I did not want to die anymore. I did not want to waste my days in an isolated house, without the possibility of having a future, a job, and a family.

In that sick condition, on 30th September, 2002, I decided to leave my country and my family. My destination was India. I was helped by a local businessman. Moved by compassion, he gave me money that helped to facilitate my way to Lhasa and then to Nepal. The fear was constant in my heart but I did not have to face problems except those related to my body, which was too weak for those long hours of walking.

I arrived at the Tibetan reception centre in Kathmandu,[40] and four weeks later, on 28th October, I reached north India, at Dharamsala, where the Tibetan Government-in-exile is based. Here I had the great fortune to meet His Holiness the Dalai Lama twice. I did not have a private audience but a public one. On that occasion, the emanation of compassion asked if there were any political prisoners among us. I raised my hand and told him that I had spent five years in Drapchi prison. He came to me and took away all the pain with a single caress of face.

All of my life I had prayed to his picture in the dark of night, in the cold solitude of a locked room. Now he was in front of me.

Starting from nothing, in a country with different customs and traditions, a different language, a different climate, a different landscape, is not easy. However, I had to do it, like all of the Tibetans in exile. So, I started attending school again.

I was admitted to the special classes arranged for the new arrivals from Tibet, although eventually, due to my bad health, I had to give up this opportunity. The Security Department of our government-in-exile looked for another way to help me. I was assigned, as a contribution to the

---

40. Kathmandu is the capital of Nepal.

society, to the first place of reception in Nepal. It was the most desirable task I could aspire to. I gave my smiles and received many from the newcomers. A few months earlier, I had been in their condition—frightened, tired, in search of respite, and hoping for a better life. I was actually taking the role of the same man who, on my arrival as a new refugee, helped me.

Fate, however, does not always treat you kindly. In August, I was plagued by strong pains in the abdomen. At the Om Nepalese Hospital, they found I had advanced stomach cancer. I was operated and sent to receive advanced treatment in India. I had six cycles of chemotherapy and now I am being treated by a doctor in this town. I feel better, although I have many restrictions to ensure that I maintain a good state of health.

Since 27th September, 2002, I have been a member of the executive centre of the Gu-Chu-Sum movement.

He is proud, you can read it from the expressions in his face.

I was democratically elected twice in a row!

How can this stranger be so calm?

I ask him if I can take a picture to attach to his story and he, as if he was an innocent child, settles in his chair and stiffens in order to look better in the picture. I start shooting and hurriedly get ready to go out of this building and get some air. I stop by Soepa[41] (that's what he calls himself). He takes my hands, looks me in the eye and, without contacting the translator for help, says to me, *Thank you.*

'For what?'

---

41. Soepa is the proper name of this person.

The dream that I kept in the drawer of my soul, was to tell my story. Do not misunderstand my words, I'm not judging, but you must understand that here in exile everything is different from where I grew up. Here, I learned that politics exists! Oh yes, it exists and it's complicated. The Tibetan government, when it sends us abroad for the purpose of making people aware of the lack of human rights in Tibet, never chooses, never takes into consideration the true political prisoners. I do not know why. Those people are certainly more educated than me, but do they really know what it feels like to live in a Chinese prison?

Do not think I am against my government. That is not what I want to say. I do not understand the reasons, but I accept the decision because I know many things have certainly been considered and this the best for the collective benefit of the Tibetan people.

I would just like to ask you, if you can, to make the testimonies you are collecting known to other people and not to keep them just for yourself. Listen to the stories of as many people as you can. If they do not all seem alike, then everyone is entitled to give voice to their stories, because everyone has different feelings, thoughts, and emotions, and a different way of expressing how they have suffered.

It is my prayer that, even if only a few people hear your voice, you will be able to free from pain the souls who have gone through hell on earth.

He stops for a moment to recover his breath, and then continues.

So thank you, for being here, for giving me two hours of your morning, for being moved when I was talking, and thanks for reading with your eyes that which you will not forget. Memory is the most effective means of improving oneself and not falling into repeated mistakes. Everything you have heard is what has happened. Maybe if I had magnified the truth, I would have had personal benefit, but my karma, if I had made such an affront to justice, would not have given me the opportunity to start a wonderful life in India with a wife who is my life and a hope that is the beating of my heart.

I shake his hands and thank him in turn. From this moment onward, destiny will lead us to come across one another many times in the streets of McLeod Ganj and, at every opportunity, the smiles that will be on our faces will be increasingly extended, linked by a special bond, until we become friends.

Zomkyi

*M*y *name is Zomkyi.*
 She is a girl who has infinite energy. She laughs all the time, makes fun of the improvised English she is speaking, and an hour will pass while she tells me her story, jostling my shoulder each time she slips from English to Tibetan without realizing it.
 I do not know how old I am, maybe forty.
 'If you are forty, you carry the years badly!' interrupts her friend on the next bed. 'You are not forty years old! If you're forty, how old does that make me?'
 They burst out laughing.
 Today, too, I find myself at Gu-Chu-Sum.
 I'm not in the part of the building that houses the offices, the meeting rooms, and the headquarters of the movement. Next to this area there is a Japanese restaurant and, in the back, across a terrace, there is a tailor's shop and some bedrooms. The complex where the building is located is part of the association of former political prisoners.
 Today I am here in the company of two sparkling nuns who, to break the embarrassment, make fun of it.
 This typically Tibetan feature is perhaps one of the facets of these people that I like the most—the ability to react to a situation of inner blockage, taking it a little less seriously and making fun of their faults. I think it's a nuance, a most spectacular one. I find it a reaction so

opposed to the inner state that overwhelms us in that particular condition, that it becomes really effective.

Unfortunately, as a good Italian, I cannot always put it into practice.

Ok, do not write my age! She wants to be forty years. *Pretend like you did not ask about it!* The laughter continues.

I was born in a village near Lhasa, to a peasant family of nine children. I am the eldest. When I was around six years old, I attended a school where I was taught Tibetan and Chinese, but I left a few months later to help my parents to work the fields.

I spent my childhood on the family estate with brothers and sisters, animals and the countryside. It was a very rustic life, consisting of few material things and many duties. The alarm at night for the first tasks in and out of the house; a simple breakfast in the room where there was a black stove; work, work, and more work until the evening when, at sunset, we went home and ate dinner with the family, before sleep overwhelmed us. For years I have remembered this with a smile. I did not know pain in that period. It may be that the peasant life does not allow itself the luxury of thoughts that go beyond daily food and a roof to sleep under at night.

Around the age of 17, driven by admiration for a paternal uncle who was good, just, and compassionate, I made the decision to follow his destiny and become a nun. I greatly admired that quiet man who always had a caress and a word of comfort for me, even in the face of the mistakes I made. I wanted to become like him.

I decided to enter a Buddhist nunnery. My parents could not hope for a better life for me. I would always have a hot meal and my prayers would help their souls in this and other lives.

Tibet is a different place from the Western world. Material wealth, daily comfort, technology, and science are not part of our simple life. It is a land in which there is more contact with mother nature than technologically created facilities. The forces that keep these people moving is their faith in the teachings of Buddha, and their valuable humane traditions.

A life devoted to prayer and to the service of the Dharma is the true source of pride and well-being for a family in Tibet. This also assured the total support from relatives and friends for my chosen path. They would have two hands less to work in the fields but they would gain positive thoughts for dealing with the problems that emerge in samsara.

The monastery to which I went to start my life as a young nun was very simple and humble. The older sisters told me that before 1965—the year when it was destroyed and then rebuilt—our little nunnery was a house of extraordinary splendour. Now, it was just a common monastery where many Communist and few Buddhist teachings were imparted.

Despite this, I knew who His Holiness was. When they felt that nobody was spying on them, the older and braver nuns told us about His Holiness, who truly was a legend, to keep us going. One day, on one of these occasions, a nun told us that this 'god' was actually a man who lived a few hundred kilometres away from us.

Naturally, we felt a strong desire to see him since we also wanted to instil in us the same faith that arose in our older sisters when they talked about His Holiness. On the other hand, we also wanted a good education. We also wanted to grow under the guidance of the great lamas.

A simple life never comes without a dose of ignorance. We did not know the reality of the world that was different from ours, and so, without thinking of the dangers it would entail, driven only by a desire to have access to what is considered *true knowledge for us, we started small demonstrations by circumambulating the monastery. We did not even have posters, only our voices, asking for religious freedom, to have access to spiritual guides so that we can practically succeed in our inner journey of spiritual attainment that ultimately matures into full enlightenment.*

The Chinese police took away our identity documents, although they were not like the documents that common Chinese citizens possess. Still, they were all that we had officially. They were simple ID cards in which our lower rank as Tibetans was clearly printed, in sharp contrast to the documents and passports that Han Chinese enjoyed.

However, we did not stop voicing our hopes. The punishment of no longer having an identity card issued by the Chinese Government was not really a great loss. So one day—I do not remember the year—a group of people (nuns, monks, and lay people) began to walk around the great temple called Jokhang, convinced that the risk was worth taking. I also joined the demonstration. It was a question of what was more important, my own safety or the future of our country. To me, the future of our country was far more important than a simple life of one individual like me, even if it was a life with every luxury in the world.

If seen from the Chinese eyes, we were breaking the law. But that law was illegally and forcibly imposed on us by our foreign invaders. Walking in groups of more than two people is considered a crime in Tibet. We gave no heed to the law, but started our demonstration calling for freedom for the land of snow. That morning, on the sacred path of the kora,[42] there were several hundred people, walking and praying. Our demonstration lasted about ten minutes before

---

42. *Kora* literally means 'to go around'. Here it describes the external path that runs around and encloses a temple.

it was violently attacked by Chinese soldiers. Sometime in the melee, I fainted and became unconscious.

I felt pain and woke up in a police station to an interrogation. 'Who started the protest?' 'If you tell us who the leader is and we'll let you out.' But there were no organizers or leaders. I tried to explain this, but they did not believe me. 'You do not understand anything about freedom, about the Dalai Lama. Tell us who is behind all this?'

There were four of them. As they beat me in that room, I realized that all the truth I had was not going to make them stop. I heard loud shouts and cries from the adjacent rooms.

Their favourite game was to handcuff me, hang me on the wall and let me spin, using kicks and punches as the engine of that spinning movement. My whole body hurt during that game. They cleaned my blood with spittle and cold water. Then they dumped me in an isolation cell until the next day, at six in the morning, when everything started all over again—the same questions, the same beatings, and the same threat: 'If you do not tell us who are the organizers and leaders, you will be in jail for a long time.'

One of my colleagues received a nine-year sentence, others eight and three.

It was 14th October when I first entered the prison where I stayed for two-and-a-half years—at the Gutsa.[43] The conditions of this prison were really bad. Men, women, the elderly, the sick, and the healthy, all were mixed up. The food was served through a crack and consisted of the same menu for the all three meals—a small piece of bread with hot water,

---

43. Gutsa, also known as 'No. 4 Unit', is a detention centre where inmates are imprisoned without a sentence. Known for its terrible conditions, it is located three miles east of Lhasa.

and this only on days of good fortune, as sometimes they forgot that it was time for us to eat. If we screamed, 'We're hungry!' they responded by kicking us in the stomach.

We could not pray. If they found out we did, our prayers would bring us more torture.

Winter in Tibet is really cold, and unbearable if you're dressed only in rags. The cold becomes your worst enemy. In addition to this, if you were unlucky, you would be given a cell where there was a passage for cold water, with guards who did not recognize you as a human being. They put us in such cells in order to punish us, or they made us do a hundred turns around the fence, barefoot in the snow.

There was a policewoman. I still remember her face. She was really bad. Although a Tibetan like us, we heard that she was sold as a child to some Chinese. Except her blood, the Chinese had taken everything she would have inherited as a Tibetan—her mother language, her compassion, and everything that defines us as Tibetans. It was all missing in her.

One night she heard us talk about her, took my friend, made her lie down on the ground and put her to sleep by trampling her head and kicking her on the mouth. We had to hide our friend from the other jailers for a whole day. If they had come to know the condition she was in, using the excuse of a medical check-up, they would have taken her life, along with litres of her blood, to be used to treat patients in Chinese hospitals.

Considering that the most coveted moments were the hours when we had to clean up one-month-old faeces with our bare hands—it was the only moment when we could go out into the open air—life in Chinese prison was truly similar to experiencing hell on earth. The memories are alive and clear in my mind, as if all this *happened yesterday. Even today, I relive the smells, the flavours, the sounds of it all in my sleep, like a film set on replay.*

I spent the last six months of my imprisonment in a different prison—the Trisam[44] *prison. Here the conditions were better. According to the Chinese policy, this prison is an educational centre, and this meant that I could move up a level, leaving the hell of Gutsa to the new arrivals. According to the evaluation of the Chinese, I had understood the crime for which I had been imprisoned. I left the place of torture to others and I could devote myself to a lot of work at Trisam, with little time to think and suffer.*

I was released suddenly, in what seems like the blink of an eye. I wanted to go back to my old nunnery but I could not. Having been a political prisoner, I was kept isolated even in freedom. I stayed six months in my native home but then, unable to settle down, I went to the nunnery. The desire to continue my spiritual journey brought me back for a few weeks to wearing red robes and shaving my head. But everyone was too scared that the Chinese would discover me there. I had to leave with the warning from the police station that if I left my home again, I would go back to prison.

On 27th September, 1995, I made the decision to come to India.

Tsering stops the story with eyes wide open. '1995? I also made the trip at that time!' he says. They smile, and the bald lady sitting on the bed next to him, caresses his cheek.

---

44. Trisam is the name of the prison known to house the excess prisoners of Drapchi and Gutsa. Located a few miles from Lhasa, it is made up of three sections—one for political prisoners, one for political crimes and one for men, for minor crimes.

I escaped with a group of three other nuns. We walked for 20 nights through the snow-capped mountains to Nepal. I arrived in Dharamsala on 25th October, and a month later I became an inmate at a new nunnery at the foot of the mountain that supports this city.

Before that day, however, I had the greatest fortune of my life. I went to His Holiness and felt so many blessings upon coming in his presence. I was amazed at my luck to see His Holiness in person, but at the same time while being happy for myself, I felt sorry for many others in Tibet who so desperately wanted to see His Holiness at least once in their life. Finally, I had before my eyes the emanation of compassion, smiling upon me. But when it occurred to me that many people would never get this chance, I felt this great emotion.

I have been here, hosted by this association, for six months while I attempt to learn English. I have lessons every morning, and in the afternoon we study together.

She indicates her two companions and two other friends who, all this while, have sat on the floor, listening to the story.

I do not have time to ask any questions, for the other nun raises her hand and says, 'It's my turn!'

Zomkyi replies that I must be surely tired and now it was time for a break. She wants to eat the cookies on the table but, if we were not present and if we were not the first to start what would be like a feast for her, it is not possible for her to have the snack.

We stop for a few minutes. We do not have time to take rest, as the girl in front of me invites us to follow her into her English class. She does not want to be disturbed by the noise of the sisters.

Sonam Dicky

I come from a village near Lhasa and I am 41 years old.
She winks.

My family is special, even for the Tibetan world. There are four of us, two sisters and two brothers. We have all taken the way of the monastery.

I decided to become a nun at the age of 12. I did not know anything about Buddhism but I remember one day my mother took me to hear a prayer. I sensed something special and unforgettable. I was completely captivated by those deep voices and the sound of trumpets, as if I was in a trance of peace and tranquillity. I floated in a dimension different from the real world. I wanted to experience this feeling as often as possible, so I found my path to a nunnery.

My illusions and my dreams of infinity immediately proved false. I did not study religion. I increased my spirit of goodness and compassion, but I was given only Communist terms and Communist ideas to feed my mind with. Fortunately, my brothers and sisters, natural and spiritual, were not afraid to explain the truth to me. At the age of 15 I knew who His Holiness the Dalai Lama was. I knew he was in India and why he had to choose exile.

In addition, I had an enquiring mind and I could not find a genuine reason why there were many who died every day, leaving their family members behind—mothers without children, wives without husbands, and children without parents. Those who died were persecuted simply because they *did not comply with the orders of the Chinese conquerors, and chose not to forget their origin and faith.*

That was my inspiration to join the protest. A man wrote posters saying, 'Long live the Dalai Lama! Freedom!' And we hung them up three times outside the monastery and on the walls of Chinese-owned houses.

The police decided to stop us, barricading us inside the nunnery without food or water for days, convinced that this would lead us naturally to oppose and hate the one we were suffering for—our true leader, who was in exile.

We rebelled and did not give up. At the age of 23, I was arrested and imprisoned for three months. It was winter, 1993.

The punishment that I had to endure was a very bitter one. If I did not answer during the interrogation, they would throw cold water on me. At that time of the year in Lhasa, the outside temperature would reach minus 15 degrees. When the water touches the body, it was like a blade of ice. I remember that, to warm myself, I would tear my clothes and make small balls that I would then tie together—it was the rosary with which I counted the prostrations.

At that time, my prayer was the only source of my warmth. I did not really care whether I lived or died. I was totally indifferent. The only thing that mattered to me was the reason why these soldiers punished my body. I believe it was the great belief in my human rights that made me endure this torture. I would never have left my ideal. I was ready for whatever was waiting for me. I knew this before I had decided to make my voice heard. I knew my protest would be followed by imprisonment, torture, and even death. I was as much ready for death as I was for torture. Everyone knew what the Chinese would do if we protested against them.

When they beat me, the only thought that I tried to keep close to my heart was that I was not the only one to suffer. Everyone feels pain of different kinds at some stage of their life.

When I was released, I went to my home, but the police were waiting for me. They took away the key of my room and gave me the news that, with the choice I had made, I had also lost my home—it now belonged to the Peoples' Republic of China. The real problem was that I could not even go to the nunnery or else I would spend the next three years in jail.

Because of my involvement in the political resistance against the Chinese rule in Tibet, my siblings were also targeted and faced similar fate as me. The Chinese soldiers ransacked their rooms, in the three different monasteries where they lived. The Chinese found three Tibetan flags and three photos of the Dalai Lama. My siblings were hunted due to my involvement in the political movement.

We lived for a year-and-a-half together in our former family home, without being able to wear monastic clothes, and with the obligation to go every month to the police station to show that we were present in the place established by the Chinese security department, and to refresh our memory of the right conduct we should have. On one of these visits I was offered an exchange—if I renounced religion, protests, and denied the Dalai Lama publicly, I would be able to enjoy a livelihood with the support of the government, with financial stability and a greater freedom of movement. In short, a much more comfortable life than the one I was living.

My decision was clear, both in my mind and in my heart. In 1997, I left Tibet and my whole family.

When I arrived in Nepal, after five days in a Nepalese prison, I was given the news that my father had died. On the way to Dharamsala, I learnt that my mother had also followed him.

I was the only one of my siblings who managed to reach exile. The others are still in Tibet, without a proper home and without any monastery. They cannot follow me for two main reasons. Firstly, they do not have any financial means to bear the expenses to pay for a guide to take them on the less risky route to Nepal. Secondly, as they have already been recognized as dissidents by the Peoples' Republic of China, if something went wrong on the way, or if they were caught on the road to freedom, they would either be tortured endlessly or would be killed instantly.

In exile, I have opportunities that would be impossible if I had stayed back in Tibet. Here, I can pray, I can study and I can walk freely. And I have also learnt again how to be happy.

Although sadness and the memory of my suffering are in my heart, deeply rooted, the impact of the Buddhist teachings on impermanence and the conviction that these feelings do not last long is very helpful for me in dealing with my past memories.

In addition to my story, I would also like to offer you something else, some advice. I would like to give you a precious key that I used to conquer the bitter tears. I am saying this so that others do not have to experience the most painful time in order to arrive at this simple truth.

Always remember that even when you have experienced negative situations, this does not mean that you will never live in joy and cherish yourself.

I see in most people, especially those who, like you, travel from the West, a desperate and periodic search for happiness that lies outside, in the material world, in the body. I see you lose yourself in the rage and the rancour of the past or in an endless planning for the future, but never really stopping your quest and being contented in the present.

You seek so much outside of you without realizing that true tranquillity starts from what we are now—in our present and our spirit—not in buds that still have to bloom or in memories that no longer exist. How can one think of living anchored to what has already existed for some time or still has to sprout?

How can one be convinced that happiness is not something that comes from the outside, work, or economic well-being? It would take so little to understand that the exterior is not something to be counted on for a peace that resides within, if only we could look at things rationally, without falling under the influence of emotions. There will always be other people who, whether they want to or not, will cause us suffering. There will always be new obstacles in our path, but how can we overcome new ones if we still dwell in past resentments? Our inability to overcome the challenges of life comes from our reluctance to accept the truth that suffering is a part of our life.

The secret lies only in letting go of excessive planning and a past that is no longer a part of us. It is good to view one's life as if it was a plain blue sky with random flashes of clouds that bring pain. The secret is to see the clouds and yet to dwell in the serene blue, instead of dwelling on what could contaminate that sky. The key that I give you for happiness is the fact that everything depends on your ability to change your way of thinking.

This is the core of the teaching for which I have protested so that it can be preserved. It is the result of studying the words of the Buddha and listening to the voice of His Holiness.

What I would like for my future is to study as much as I can and help others. I will not be able to do that on a monetary level—I am aware that I will never have the finances to be able to sponsor the livelihood of anyone. But I believe there are other ways I can be helpful. I can give advice, give smiles, and alleviate the suffering of others through my experience and the lessons I have learned.

I would like to talk of those people who have sacrificed their lives for the Tibetan cause, using fire—self-immolations. This year I think we have already reached 40 self-immolations.[45] *Life is precious. If you want to fight for freedom you have to be strong, steady, intelligent, and have an education, and only through this can you really fight.*

I would like to talk to them. How I wish His Holiness could return home, so that all this would end. He has every right to live among us and we have every right to be able to grow under his leadership. There is a stark difference in the personality of those who have grown under His Holiness as against those who have grown under the political influence of China. A personality developed through His Holiness' leadership knows forgiveness and compassion while the Chinese government seems to be encouraging the opposite.

We have the truth on our side. Tibet is a free country and it isn't and has never been a part of China. The Dalai Lama is our spiritual leader, he comes from Tibet, and he must return.

No? She asks me with wide eyes.

I smile and nod.

I have the same thoughts as she has in her heart. I lack only this strength to smile so purely after such immense pain.

---

45. At the time of writing this book, the number of self-immolations in Tibet has crossed 170.

LT

I usually have lunch and dinner in a tavern on McLeod's market street. It is certainly not the most suitable place for foreigners, with a menu consisting strictly of Tibetan food, iron tables, and uncomfortable and greasy chairs. The height however, has always attracted me. Although I am troubled by a fear of heights, here I am surrounded by glass walls and sheltered by a roof—this atmosphere has always benefited the process of transformation of ideas into words. In addition, this is the meeting point of all my friends, the difference being that they are all Tibetans while I am not.

Before being able to get a little closer to the young people who work in this little restaurant, it took months for them to get accustomed to the features of my face. Only after weeks of continuous acquaintance did they begin to treat me as one of them and less and less like the usual *inji*.[46] This included a service upgrade that I wished had not happened—now the food is even more difficult for me. I'm not served first and sometimes I get ignored until I'm the one to ask for the menu.

This treatment has, however, some positive aspects. Now that they know my name, they stop for a few words. One day, spontaneously, one of them, after knowing what my work consists of, decides to contribute with his own memories. The only two conditions he has

---

46. *Inji* means 'foreigner' in Tibetan.

are quite simple—he will tell me his story in a place not frequented by Tibetans, and some parts with some secrets should not be reported on paper.

It is a Sunday morning and we find ourselves sitting down to breakfast at 8 o'clock. The boy has only the mornings free.

My name is LT. I was born in 1984, maybe 1985. In my document it is written that I am 27 years old, but I am confused about my age. I come from the Kham region, a rural area of the Tibetan plateau. It is in the south-east, bordering China—the land of the warriors of Tibet.

Of my childhood I have only vague memories. As far as I remember, I have always been wearing monk's robes. Since our family consisted of several children—we were five, three boys and two girls—I was given to the monastery in my childhood. This is customary in Tibet. If you have several children, then one is entrusted to the Dharma in order to contribute to the spiritual well-being of the family and all sentient beings.

I'm the only member of my family in India right now. I arrived in India at an early age. Even my parents do not know where I am. There is only one person from my hometown who knows about me. That person is a relative.

I do not know for what strange reason, perhaps some mental block or psychological defence mechanism might be involved in this, but my conscious memories begin with my journey between Tibet and India. Anything that happened before that moment is just a black hole that my thoughts cannot illuminate.

We went to Lhasa by road and walked from the capital to Nepal. It took us a month and ten days to reach Nepal. We did the journey in two groups—15 people in one, 22 in the other. We travelled together but we ate separately.

When we arrived in Nepal, we were arrested by the local police who gave us two alternatives—pay five thousand Nepalese rupees and they would deliver us to the Tibetan reception or else we would be handed over to the Chinese. Our group took three days to make a decision.

There were three other kids with us, but I was the smallest. They started explaining to me that we would go separately once we reached India. The children would not come to the monastery with me but would go to school. I asked the group leader several times if I could go with them to study at TCV—I did not have the slightest idea why I was wearing the yellow and red robes and I had never taken any vows. But he had no choice. He had to deny me the opportunity others would enjoy because he had assured my family that he would entrust me to a monastery. He could not change his word just because of my desire, which was without foundation.

My destiny took me to the monastery of Gaden Jangtse in the south of India. Here there were two types of schools. In one, besides Buddhism, English, history, and mathematics were taught. This was attended by the children of Tibetans born in India. In the other, where I was enrolled, Dharma was studied in the Tibetan language.

My studies were slow. I started at the beginners' level, yet the books I was given contained notions of levels too deep to be understood by those who did not know the previous steps. Buddhism is a great medicine. To benefit from it, you need to start with small doses and then move on to serious medication. If you do not follow this process, you could lose yourself.

I lost myself. With sadness in my heart, I can now say that I lost myself during the only occasion that life ever offered me to heal from the suffering given by my feelings. I took the wrong streets—streets of envy—for a false freedom that was denied to me. My ego did not allow me to be free from being envious of those who lived in the world outside the monastery, instead of studying and practising towards enlightenment. I lost myself at a young age through a decision that did not arise in my heart but that I always felt was forcing me, limiting and compelling me.

That was not the only problem I had to face.

When my companions and I went out of the monastery for a walk, for small purchases, they were in a position to communicate and understand everything. As I only knew the Tibetan language and remained within the boundaries of my own culture, I was unable to interact with others. When I wanted to buy a shampoo, I spent hours looking at the products, not being able to read the labels to identify what I needed. Many times I went back to my room with things that I did not need. In the end I gave up trying to carry on with my own limited understanding and decided to buy what others were buying.

The pride in me, which did not allow me to ask for a friend's help in dealing with a clear inability, has always plagued me. With time, embarrassment about being so different and often feeling inept, increased. It would have been much easier if I had not been overcome by those feelings.

In 2008, I made the decision to leave the monastery. At first I went to Jaipur in Rajasthan,[47] where I worked for a businessman who sold clothes. I stayed there for a year. Then I went to Delhi where I tried my luck in a call centre. My friends who worked there earned in 20 nights what I managed to earn after three months of hard work. Many companies would not hire me because I did not know English. A mere knowledge of Dharma and Tibetan does not open many doors when it comes to finding work. Fortunately, a friend who lived in the Tibetan

---

47. An Indian state near Delhi.

settlement in Bylakuppe[48] and owned a travel agency took me in despite my communication constraints.

All this while I kept in touch with my family in Tibet. It will be years before I find the courage to tell them of the great difficulties I encountered outside the monastery. It was not necessary to confess it in words. My father asked me to come home. To him my stay in India made no sense.

I tried to reach Tibet illegally in 2011. Between Nepal and my country there is a bridge that separates the two nations, but it is impossible to cross it without help. We paid one hundred thousand Indian rupees to a Nepalese guide, who assured me of safe passage once we reached the other side. He lied to me. The Chinese police were waiting for me. They stripped me, handcuffed me, and interrogated me with questions like: 'Why do you come and go without permission?' 'How long have you been in India?' 'You have been instructed by the Dalai Lama. With what right do you now come back to the Chinese soil?' 'You look poor. Where are your blessed things?'

I look at him and interrupt.'Please explain what they meant by *blessed things*.'

They're things that you are also wearing right now. First of all, the red thread,[49] *blessed by His Holiness, which represents the connection with what our spirituality calls.*

---

48. Bylakuppe is located in the south of India, in the state of Karnataka, and is home to one of the largest Tibetan settlements in India.
49. The red thread has a knot in the middle. It is at this point that a Lama touches it to bless it. It is worn on the neck or on the left arm/wrist (the right hand is used for the dirtiest tasks). When the thread breaks, it must be placed in a clean place, identified according to tradition as a monastery, or hung from a tree. Inside the bags given with the thread, there are hundreds of small pills called *mani rilbu*. Three of these pills should be taken after washing oneself in the morning. These little pills, before being given to the people, remain in His Holiness' monastery for months and receive the prayers which they now contain within them.

The most important thing that the soldiers try to find, but rarely succeed in, is the tson-soong.[50]

I get lost during these stories, so different from the tranquillity in which I grew up. The more they speak, the more enthusiasm arises in me to understand all their intricacy in greater detail.

My ears hear the words, but sometimes I miss the sense they carry. It seems like an insurmountable problem. Learning sounds and their literal meanings helps little when the culture they represent is not appreciated in spirit by the listener. A genocide has taken place. I see a people who have been massacred and yet they remain calm, as if untouched. I see youths without families, without economic possibilities, without external help to grow. They lack the basic necessities of food and shelter, but nevertheless succeed in making sure that life is stronger than the feeling of powerlessness to change their condition. I see people who, in order not to betray their beliefs, have stripped themselves of everything and continue to place the core of their existence in prayer and faith.

There are moments when I wonder what I would have done if I had been in their place. If I would have been so faithful after finding myself in a different land, where I am a guest and not a master, with nothing but the company of those in my same condition. I am not

---

50. *Tson-soong* is an object or amulet for protection. There are several of these, all very powerful. Those with the greatest power of protection are said to be given by His Holiness the Dalai Lama or His Holiness the Karmapa. Inside, scrolls with many tantric mantras are enclosed over which, for days and days, monks and lamas have prayed. You cannot open the *tson-soong* and they must be kept in clean places. They protect against all kinds of danger but if they are not treated with proper respect, they are said to be dangerous.

sure how I would have survived all this. Tibet and its people are so rich in rituals that an Italian finds it difficult to grasp. They are still so tied to the impalpable, so intertwined with almost shamanic movements, so full of superstitions and beliefs, that an unaccustomed eye runs the risk of not noticing.

The blessed objects that are kept safe at the cost of one's life are symbols that the Chinese themselves deny, being atheists, but yet they seek them as treasures of inestimable value.

In this situation, it is useless to use reason to try to understand the sense of their life-force. I hear a voice within my spirit that whispers to me that the key will be given only when I learn those concepts myself and, on another level—certainly not a conventional one—I will let this community teach my unconscious spirit what it means.

Then they continued with questions and threats.'Give us information about the government-in-exile if you want to live.' 'Are you a spy for Lobsang?'[51] 'Did you vote?'

I did not answer their questions. They would have beaten me anyway. They would not believe me and even if my fate had been different, my loyalty still went where my heart was—to His Holiness the Dalai Lama, in India.

The first prison that housed me for seven days was between the Nepalese and Chinese border. Every day the routine was the same, but the people who conducted the interrogation changed. They focused more and more on the subject of self-immolations. 'Do you think these men are martyrs of the

---

51. Lobsang Sangye is the Tibetan Prime Minister of the exiled government based in Dharamsala.

nation?' And they asked about the Kalachakra.[52] *For them it was not a religious but a political gathering with dissident purpose.* 'How many people participated?' Understanding that I was just a boy and useless for their purpose, they moved me to Nyelam prison for four days.

It was so cold it forced me to wrap my body in a bedspread full of urine and blood that lay in the few square feet where I was locked up. The real problem was that for me there was neither food nor water available. I managed to survive only with the help of two Tibetan women who were in the cell next to mine. They had been imprisoned because they had participated in the Kalachakra—even though they were businesswomen doing business between Nepal and China. The treatment for them was better than mine. They could have visits from relatives who took care of their food, which these ladies shared with me.

My stay there, however, was short because more prisoners arrived. Two trucks full of Tibetans came in. These people had gone beyond the Chinese border with visas for Nepal, but they had not kept themselves within the permitted area— they had continued on to India, to hear, at least once in their lives, the teachings of the Dalai Lama.

---

52. *Kalachakra* is one of the main Buddhist teachings, given every two years by His Holiness. It is said that it is very important to receive it from him. According to tradition, the Buddha 'turned the wheel of the Dharma' (conferred spiritual teaching) three times, at each 'turn' communicating deeper doctrines. The first turning is dedicated to the four noble truths—suffering, the origin of suffering, the cessation of suffering, and the path that leads to liberation.
The second turning is dedicated to emptiness, and its essence is captured in the *Heart Sutra*, the *Prajnaparamita*, which explains the absence of intrinsic existence of phenomena. The third cycle of teachings was conferred by the Buddha in various locations in India and codified in a group of texts called *Tantra*. In Dhanyakataka, in southern India, he initiated the tradition of king Suchandra, of the mystical kingdom of Shambala, who received the esoteric teaching of the Buddha called the *Kalachakratantra*, 'the tantra of the wheel of time'.

I was transferred to Shigatse Prison for two months. There too, I was joined by trucks-loads of Tibetans. Only three men among them had any real relationship with India. Their stories were similar to mine. The others had all gone with the sole purpose of listening to Buddhist teachings for a couple of days. However, in Chinese law, they had committed a crime. Even if they had a visa for Nepal, they did not have permission to go elsewhere. For those who did not have a visa, their crime was that they had left the Chinese territory without permission.

Before entering the prison, they were all stripped of the sacred objects they wore. There were two reasons for this—to remove any link with the community in exile and to prevent suicides. The prisoners were then sorted, with women on one side and men on the other.

During these months, the daily ritual was the same for everyone—questions and beatings, beatings and questions. 'Why did you attend the Kalachakra?' 'It's just a meeting for the separation of the country.' 'The Dalai Lama is just a criminal.'

Their work on me was, instead, to reconstruct my story and find my family. I believed they succeeded in their intent. I had no doubt about it. This awareness broke inside me and, although for now my loved ones have not received any repercussions, I continue to be terrified of losing them, too. I cannot be sure that their well-being is assured in the future. The Chinese police are constantly changing strategy and maybe now they're not interested in my family, but tomorrow they could be.

My questioning was getting more and more in-depth every day. 'Do you know anyone who works for the Tibetan Government or the Dalai Lama?' 'Give us their phone numbers and their names and we will offer them an excellent job if they return to Tibet. They will have employment, a great salary, and many privileges.' 'What is Tenzin Gelek to the people?' This person is a spiritual guide from my region, and for me, for us, he is almost like His Holiness—a god on earth. Now he, too, is locked up in a Chinese prison.

'Have you ever protested?' 'Do you know about the associations in India that deal with the liberation movement of Tibet?' 'Who is a part of them? Who finances them?' 'Did they ask you to sacrifice your body for the Tibetan cause?'

Of those moments, I hold in my heart the memory of anger. My answers were filled with bitterness, not from just the taste of the blood flowing from my mouth as a result of being kicked and punched.

The stories told by those who had been in Chinese prisons before me were all true. I experienced with my body and saw with my own eyes all that was told to me in India. The truth made my heart heavy for a long time. I responded to everything in an affirmative, contemptuous manner, ignoring the pain, with a thrust of rebellion that even overcame the fear of death. I said, 'Gelek is our lama and for us that is all. I protested and distributed leaflets that praised the separation. I would set myself on fire now for the cause of my people.'

My rebellious spirit was obviously not appreciated. Perhaps silence would have earned me fewer injuries and fewer scars. For these answers, my back had to bear chairs being broken on it; I fainted so many times that I lost count.

They would have done all the torture anyway. When I answered that I did not know the associations or the people who ran them, and when exhausted I let the truth flow out that I was just a worthless boy without knowledge of anything, unable to survive in exile, they called me a liar. The mere fact that I had grown up in India, in their eyes, was proof that I held great information. They could not accept that I was a nobody, neither in Tibet nor in India.

One of the punishments I hated to receive was the punishment of lying on an upturned chair. On one leg of this chair I had to rest my head, on the opposite side my feet, and on the other two I had to hold my hands. In that position my back was completely arched and after an hour, in that position, the blood began to come out of all the points of my body that were pressing on the legs of the chair. Every time I lasted out at most two hours and then fainted. For this I had to skip a meal. If you consider that the food in prison is served twice a day—if you are lucky—then you can understand what it meant to not have dinner. In general, however, they nourished us towards one in the afternoon with a little stale tsampa,[53] and in the evening with rice.

When I fainted, being without food was not the only consequence. When I woke up on my bed, my companions had to ring the cell bell because they were told to do so if they did not want to have the same thing done to them. The soldiers then returned and brought me back to the chair.

How could they believe someone sent me as a spy? I had no money and no education. I just wanted to see my family again.

After two months of imprisonment they gave me a unique alternative. If I wanted to stay in Tibet, I had to serve three more years in prison. But if I did not want this fate, returning to India was the only solution. I had no interesting answers for them and if I stayed, I could create problems—talk to people and tell them about the freedom and rights that existed in exile. I was literally thrown out of China to the Nepalese

---

53. *Tsampa* is typical Tibetan food. It is made of barley flour to which is added hot water or milk/tea, yak cheese, and sugar. It is not cooked but eaten raw.

land. They gave me an Indian visa and sent me with the threat that if I ever returned, I would spend my whole life between one prison and another, with the certainty of an early death.

Sometimes I remember my family, especially my mother. I do not remember her face, I do not remember her touch, but there are times when I believe I can feel it.

Now, I work in a job for 4,500 rupees a month (68 Euros) and I live with a friend in his room because I am not able to pay my own rent. The money comes and just gets spent quickly. But I do not suffer. I hope one day to be able to go abroad and to afford not only a house but also a family.

I turn off the recorder. A boy so young, marked by a story, a fate that I cannot even write down. and the sense of impotence and helplessness that comes from it. In contrast were my complaints, when I grew up in the protection and fortune of a crystal castle.

We are going to get up from the plastic table that has hosted us these hours. We are about to resume a normal life, aware of how my normalcy is a dream denied to one too many.

He stops me and bids me with advice and a request.

Dadrun, be careful with your questions. Dharamsala is full of Chinese spies. They are Tibetans who are like us outwardly. They pray, they speak the same language, they go to the temple and to the market, but their intentions are not the same as ours. I ask you to remember that today we are sitting at the same table and we are friends, but maybe one day things will be different. That day I beg you, do not hurt me by revealing the things that you do not have to write, and use my story against me.

I have unconsciously absorbed something in these months. I take the photo of His Holiness and touch it to the crown of my head as a sign of promise.

There is no greater oath and we both know it.

Visual Testimonies

Sometimes, without wanting it, there comes a time when fate shows you, with the force of the power of reality, the objects[54] of torture of the red state.

It is incredible how some objects can bring out, in some moments of life, what they would not bring out in others. I would not have thought that these things, even though they were implements of pain and fear, could touch a part of the spirit of someone who observes them through the glass of the container they are kept in. It was the fastest connection that my mind had ever made. In these objects I saw the faces of the people I had interviewed for this project so far. Their words and feelings convinced me every day that these people are more and more mine, and it made my knees wobble and my stomach queasy.

As I shared their reality, it brought overwhelming emotions that I did not know I possessed. It shook the certainty of what had been, until then, my own little reality. Being challenged, and having the strength to accept the most complicated challenge, the challenge of changing oneself, required an energy that I thought I lacked. And yet, leaving aside the doubts and uncertainties I carried inside me, leaving aside the fear, I was filled with something new and overpowering.

---

54. On display at the Tibet Museum, adjacent to the temple of His Holiness the Dalai Lama, where the history of the Tibetan people, the occupation by China, and testimonies are preserved.

In another way, I vibrate with their vibrations when they are reborn from their ashes. I feel the power of the change that pulsates in my veins and makes me re-create, drawing on a new source. I perceive life and its strength in giving impulse when we thought we no longer possessed fuel in our own tank.

I do this in the form of a mirror in which I draw from the reflection of lives that I have not experienced, each different, and all characterized by this incredible energy to defeat death, to embrace a new ray of light and to be re-created, after going through hell, stronger and more untouchable than before.

This is my tribute to the memories that should not be forgotten.

Future Memories

17th August, 2017

My journey through memories is taking me further and further back, deeper and deeper into myself.

I was a little blonde girl, with dark green eyes, strong but sick, marked with a weak body and fears that God only knows how they originated, sitting in a car with my mother, full of tears from the fear of being abandoned. My parents were full of affection, united, smiling and always with the fruit of their love.

I was forever lying in different hospitals, with high fever and pain in my bones. Yet I was strong and smiled as I ran through the meadows, playing with any creature I found.

I was born in a crystal castle—beautiful, rich, and bright, but broken by a lively intelligence that filtered through the glass and made me aware and fearful of the untruths that surrounded me. I had no reason for those fears; there were no factors that could create them, at least not in this life.

My dreams spoke to me, even then. I found a piece of crumpled paper on which I had written my clichéd thoughts:

I remember a dream of my first few years of life. A drop of terror, a nightmare that haunted my nights. It was a wish that could have come true, that spoke of family and infinity. I had people, who had given me life and love, by my side, at the idyllic age of 14. I prayed that time would stop in that image of happiness; I whispered every night to the universe to never take it away. That picture used to last a few seconds. It used to come to me, clear—the awareness that my father and mother would soon fly away. I imagined myself walking toward the old, massive wooden cupboard, opening the drawer, extracting the largest blade, and following them. It was a wish, it was a terror, it was the story of a life yet to be lived.

Some call these premonitory dreams, others, coincidences. I believe that sensitive spirits already know the road they will travel on. When you are young, when your mental constructions are still weak, when you still don't have the mark of a social structure drawn by labyrinths of thought, you outline the routes that your soul must follow. So, when I was three-years-old, the only real terror that enveloped me was of being left alone, abandoned. I would have preferred to die.

I did not know that death would be to live every day. I did not know that those fears were a mirror, a moment, a vision of a mark.

Of those young years, I remember a Christmas Eve when, with my father, I had the courage to burn my pacifier. But now that I'm talking about it, I understand that I have never really left it, while I bite the pen I hold in my fingers.

I remember that my illness had almost disappeared. I remember the dream of flying and falling. I remember that when my parents disappeared from my dreams, I thought of reaching for the drawer of knives and thought to follow them.

This is the first time I am confessing all this.

I remember being eight years old when the fear of losing them began to become a reality.

I have wondered many times how to explain the fears of a child who does not know anything about the world yet. I sit, covering the events of a life, remembering the terror in the heart of a young girl in her teens, who did not know anything that could create such ideas. I've wondered, and in the end I am convinced that they were about future events.

Let me explain. I was born in a Christian country, into a Catholic family. I had my first experience of Islam at a young age; I studied Judaism and Hinduism at university; and then, at the age of 21, I embraced Buddhism, incorporating it into my daily routine. I want you to know that now I pray for nothing and I pray for all.

I have a pantheon of all the gods in my mind and in my heart. They don't overlap nor contradict one another; they coexist without clashing. How is that possible, one being God, the Creator, and the other based on the rejection of a Creator? How is it possible to have no contradiction, if one idea develops the idea of a distant God while the other has the belief that God is within us and, if cultivated, can take us out of the endless cycle of suffering to enter the realm of peace and the total vision of a Buddha?

I never understood how this coexistence of seemingly incompatible concepts is possible. But this is my everyday life and the reality of my spirit, which believes in everything, or perhaps does not believe anything but still keeps a complete faith in whatever the ultimate truth is.

This little digression about my beliefs is just to bring us to the subject of future memories. Whether I approach them as a Christian and think about an immortal soul, or whether I do this as a Buddhist, according to whom the soul does not exist and during the reincarnation, what appears to be the soul is a mental continuum, this leads me to be convinced that before birth—let's call it, for convenience, the 'soul'— the soul has the opportunity to choose.

If you think with an Asiatic mind-set, I don't see a contradiction with the idea of karma. We live, we die, and we enter the *bardo*—the period of 49 days after death where we are hyper-conscious to the point that, if we are able to recognize that everything that happens is a projection of our mind, we are able to obtain a better rebirth. More experienced practitioners at the highest level of the path to enlightenment are said to get enlightened in *bardo*. This is what Buddhist tantrayana says, but I am still an infant in Buddhism. After at the most 49 days in *bardo*, when the consciousness searches for a new birth, we take birth in a new form. This cycle of death and birth continues until we have obtained control over our birth through intensive meditative practice.

If I think with the Christian part of my heart, hoping not to run into heresy, I believe that God, before He sends us to this earth, shows us the outlines of the life we will face and, as He is a good and merciful father, leaves us the choice of what sort of life we want to live.

So I believe that a soul, before entering this life, faces a conscious choice. As if it stands in front of several video-clips, so to say, seeing generically different lives and conscious that it has to learn something from the life that is offered, the soul selects one, in complete free will.

Here, there are future memories that come to life. I am convinced therefore that I already know this life, unconsciously, concisely, but not the exact contents in detail, because the detailed contents are the choices made during my day-to-day living. I believe that before entering this world I saw the outline of this journey. The choice of how to react to this is very personal, never written, but I have the impression of knowing, deep inside, the outlines of what has happened and what will happen.

In short, I believe that the soul, before taking birth, chose this life, even if after taking this life-form it has forgotten the past, and even if this life involves traumatic experiences. However, I don't believe every aspect of this life is pre-destined or pre-determined for I believe there is a role of one's free will in directing this life. The soul had a choice of several lives from which it chose one that would contribute towards its internal development. This life is a result of that conscious choice, and the writing of this book that you are reading now is also because of that choice.

Here, there are future memories. This is the only way in which I can explain the dreams of a child born from love and yet terrified, with no apparent cause, by a sense of abandonment. This is how I can explain the idea of suicide in the heart of a person who came from somewhere where she had never been exposed to such an idea. This is how I can explain to myself the generic propensity of a person who seeks a soulmate of a particular type. Could it not be some unconscious residue of earlier-seen outlines that the soul is seeking in order to realize the path it came to live? When I was a child I had a desire to freeze my life at the age of 14, with my parents and a boy, in the belief that this was absolute happiness. If we zoom into the picture of the dreams of a dead mother and father, and I approaching the kitchen drawer, taking a knife, and following them, we start to have an idea of what was the basic idea in those fears. If, after many years, I tell you that at the age of 14, that little girl was deprived of her father by natural causes and of her mother by suicide, isn't there the feeling that those nightmares and thoughts were really, unconsciously, a premonition of what was going to happen? If, in addition, I inform you that there were other dreams in which high mountains, dominated by the deep sound of the praying voices of men with shaved heads, dressed in red, interfered in my Italian nights, would there be any doubt of how a child could see Tibet without ever having had contact with it?

What if I tell you that a few years later, without too much effort, I found myself translating a very delicate subject, commissioned by one of the translators of His Holiness the Dalai Lama, without having even asked for the assignment?

I believe in future memories and I believe that, based on their intensity, some of us still have a trace of them in us.

But let us get back to reality, to the present and this new writing. This thesis is helping me to heal my heart and is making me lose myself in new reflections.

Tibetan philosophy is too vast to be summed up in a few lines, and the myths and stories even more so. I will leave space for the words of an elderly woman who, one afternoon four years ago, at the temple of

His Holiness the Dalai Lama, between one *Om Mani Padme Hum*[55] and another, told me her story and those of others.

---

55. *Om Mani Padme Hum* is the most common mantra in the Tibetan world. Addressed to Thousand-armed Chenrezig, Sanskrit *Avaloketishvara* (a Bodhisattva depicted with a hundred eyes and a thousand hands to see all the suffering and help all), this is also a mantra for His Holiness the Dalai Lama, being himself an emanation of this Buddha of Compassion in the Tibetan belief.

Tenzin Lhaky

It is one of the few monsoon days when the rain does not fall as if someone was overturning drums of water on our heads. This afternoon we still get wet, but with very fine tears. We take the opportunity to go to the temple to pray a little. In this place, I'm learning the beauty of walking in the forest, turning a prayer wheel, and getting lost with the breath of the wind that makes the coloured flags flutter. I begin to appreciate the slow passage of time, slowly made movements, the sounds of nature, and the higher self that I have never experienced earlier. Always running all these years, I was breathless, fleeing from a part of me that clamoured to be expressed. I am learning the retreat, to the present and in the prayer with these people, who I will never be able to thank enough.

I have lost years in the frenzy of the Western world, too scared to rediscover the inner world. Fear and denial in every gesture made me not to notice the inner call that we all feel. I wonder if the tendency to deny this part of ourselves supports that inner break that we sometimes perceive. I speak with my experience of years of lying down in hospitals to cure unfounded illnesses, years of studying the philosophies of the mind to logically find an answer to inner questions. I wonder if all this created the habit of keeping my mind busy when I should have just walked and felt the present. I see cows grazing the green highlands, feel the moist air that rests on my face while the sun warms my clothes. I can never thank these people enough. They have taught me to think less and live more in the here, in the now, and in the present.

We walk the usual circumambulation, clockwise around the walls that protect the sacred site of the temple. Ngawang shows me a *momo-la*[56] who appears in a hurry, turning the beads of the rosary in her left hand. 'She will have a beautiful story,' suggests my friend.

When we hear her story, though, sitting in a *dhaba*[57] near our house, his conclusion will be different,. 'Remind me never to interview a *momo-la* again,' he would say.

I cannot write this story in the order in which she told it. This grandmother stopped too many times and decided to start again from the middle. She did not finish many of the sentences she began, and she had too many dreams mixed with a reality that she had not lived but wanted to live. We talked about legends rather than about real life. With her thin voice, this spirit of a girl who believed in fairies, with a face marked by wrinkles and gestures so fast that you could not believe that those aged bones could make them, has decided that her past would serve only as a framework for Tibetan myths, while she flew from era to era.

---

56. *Momo-la* is the Tibetan term for an elderly lady. It literally means 'grandmother' but, like Indians, the Tibetans address even unknown people by age and in terms of kinship—persons aged 20 years will call people around their age 'sister' or 'brother'. When the difference in age is more, the women will be called 'aunt', the men 'uncle'. Elderly men will all be grandfathers, and elderly women grandmothers.
57. *Dhaba* is the Hindi word for a roadside restaurant.

I am 84 and I was born in the same place that saw the birth of Thangtong Gyalpo.

She looks at us uncertainly and I think that our ignorance regarding this person she has mentioned makes her happy—a dream come true.

He is a yogi, like Milarepa. Do you know who Milarepa is?

We nod.

It does not matter. I will tell you his story!

Milarepa

Born with the name of Mila Thopaga in a province in the east of Tibet, adjacent to the Nepalese border, Milarepa was the greatest of all Tibetan yogis.

His family, known by the name of Josay, was of noble lineage. The childhood of the young Mila was one of wealth and riches, until the death of his father. Then, all his family wealth was seized by greedy uncles and the boy, his mother, and his sister lived as slaves for many years. Reaching the age of maturity, he tried to regain a life worthy of his position, but faced the derision of uncles. His mother, full of rancour, with the money obtained by selling half a field, begged her son to study the art of black magic with dedication to seek vengeance. The threat which she used was that if he was not able to fulfil the mission, she would choose death over life, and he would only see her corpse if he returned without having mastered the black magic.

You are young, in an age that has forgotten the connection with the universe. You believe that any form that does not have a strong and formed material body is an illusion and illness of the mind. You believe in the magic of the technology of telephones that brings voices of distant people. You are completely deceived by the rigidity of your thoughts and your mind; you forget about true human capabilities. You take as imagination any story that has spells and beings that you cannot see with your eyes, because of your blindness. But I am old and I remember when all these stories, which are now unimportant, were real and clear in everyone's hearts. When the earth was respected because it was shared with the spirits that lived there, and we lived in harmony, in a peaceful life, a life much richer than the one that exists now.

Magic exists. The spirits live, and they are beside us.

Young Mila quickly learned from Lama Yungtun-Trogyal and mastered the powers of destruction. He used them to fulfil his mother's wishes, invoking a great storm of rain and wind on the day of his cousin's wedding, destroying their home and killing 35 people. The inhabitants of the village, incensed with rage, began to search for Mila, who, warned by his mother, defended himself by invoking demons and storms that destroyed all the houses and killed most of the inhabitants. His teacher of magic, understanding with what intent the boy had studied his art, sent him away, to look for someone who could explain how to neutralize the negative karma accumulated with his actions.

Mila became the 'heart' student of Marpa Lotsawa, the translator. Before giving him lessons, Marpa had him build and destroy three towers. After this work he continued to refuse to transmit knowledge. The only way to eliminate the karma of Mila's past was for him to spend 12 years engaged in the construction of a statue of a nine storeyed building all by himself. He is said to have been the only person able to finish such a feat in the span of one life.

Thus, through years of dedicated service to his master and with strong remorse for his past negative deeds, Milarepa purified his negativities through the ordeal that he was put through by Marpa.

Marpa transmitted and entrusted a particular lineage to each of his 'heart' students. The teachings covered the illusory body, the clear light mind, the intermediate stage, dream yoga, and the transfer of consciousness. The power of the inner fire was transmitted to Milarepa. Being known as a *repa*, he wore only a thin piece of cloth that left bare most of his body.

At the age of 45, Milarepa engaged in meditation with ardour and devotion, in the cave of Dakar Taso (today known as the Cave of Milarepa), sustaining himself only on nettle soup that led to the development of mould and gave him a greenish skin colour. He achieved complete enlightenment in one lifetime.

Soon, his fame spread and many people began to seek him out to listen to the sublime songs through which he expressed his realization. He explained the crucial points of the Dharma in a simple and clear way, and poets of the later eras translated his compositions into many languages. He continued to lead a very simple life, imparting teachings to a restricted circle of 21 disciples, both male and female—8 'major' and 13 'minor' disciples.

His successor, who was concerned with continuing the tradition, was Gampopa and the monastery associated with him is in the village of Zhonggang. Today this spiritual house, consecrated and blessed by this yogi, still shines with beauty, thanks to the restoration done by Nepalese artists after the destruction.

Thang Tong Gyalpo

It is said that those born in the same places as these great yogis are blessed forever.

Ngawang and I look at each other uncertainly. Neither of us has ever heard of this, but I think it's not important, since another story is ready for us.

Thang Tong Gyalpo was born in the 14th century in Olpa Lhartse, north of Tsang. He is known by many different names, including Drubthob Chakzampa and Tsundru Zangpo. He was a great Buddhist practitioner, a yogi, an architect, and a construction engineer.

He was the builder of many stupas, among the most majestic being the Kumbum Chorten, in the monastery of Degde Gonchen, in Derge, in the state of Kham. According to belief, this stupa was erected through his spiritual powers alone. He is said to have built at least 108 bridges between Tibet and Bhutan, some of which are still in use today, that have allowed movement from one sacred area to another throughout the Himalayan region. The works to remember are many, but two stand out—the passage that opened from the aboriginal land of Kongpo on the Indian borders, so beautiful that it encouraged all the Tibetan pilgrims who wanted to visit the sacred places in Tsarito to cross the border, and the raised iron bridge of Chakzam, 65 kilometres from Lhasa, abandoned since 1948 and being replaced by another new construction located 100 metres from it. (You can still see the old bridge today, and admire it as a testimony to the glory of Tibetan civilization.)

It was this passion that earned him the name 'the Father of Tibetan Opera'. To raise the means needed for the production of his iron giants, he invented the 'dance of the seven sisters', also called known as *Ache Lhamo*, in which the performers dance and speak quickly to the rhythm of the drums. From this he got another epithet, 'the man from the empty land', and the honour of being 'the guardian of all the altars located on the stages'. Here, he is represented as an old man holding a piece of white bread. Close to all the bridges, above the walls, he is painted with a long white beard and pieces of iron.

He was awakened inwardly, acquiring the great capacity of integrating many elements of different teachings. For this reason, he is often placed in different schools of thought, even those which are opposed to each other outwardly.

When he died, some reported his age to be 124 years.

In 1949, the Chinese invaded Tibet and all the problems started. They took all our belongings, our assets became theirs, and they left us with only anger and fear. One day, my mother and uncle decided to meet in our home. The Chinese police imagined that this was a danger to them. They burst into the room and asked how many cups of tea they had been drinking (the question was for information purpose—how long had this meeting been going on?) and what arguments they had discussed. My mother and uncle responded with the truth—only two cups of bö cha[58] *between the discussions of*

---

58. *Bö cha* is the classic Tibetan tea made with milk, butter, salt, and black tea. As can be expected from the ingredients, it has a salty and very smooth taste due to the butter.

general family topics. They had nothing in mind that could harm the new government. But the consequences would have been the same even if they had drunk a dozen cups while they were planning a revolt. They took my mother's face in their hands and began to smash it against the table. Then they imprisoned her, or rather, imprisoned us.

In prison, the prisoners were divided into six groups. My mother ended up in group five. The prisoners were beaten and tortured and I listened to the tears of the woman who had brought me into the world while some policemen questioned me, 'Do you intend to follow the road that your mother is going down or to be like the other citizens?' All this refrain was repeated for a few days, always the same. The only difference was that my mother had less and less force to cry and transmit her pain.

They freed us, but from that point our true hell began. One night, a few days later, my mother did not return home. I was desperate. I left my daughter (at that time she was very young) with a neighbour and spent a whole day in the countryside, searching for her. I found her body covered with sacks between the banks and the torrent of the river.

She was not killed directly by the Chinese militia. At that time, Beijing's politics were different. They hired groups of Tibetans, promising privileges and money if they destroyed the mentality that demanded independence. The one who killed my mother was a brother of mine—not by blood, but still a brother, from the same area of Kham, part of the organization **Thru Kamba**.

I tried to pull her body from the water but it was too heavy for me. I asked the police for help. They arrived, escorted by the man who had taken my mother's life a few hours earlier and left her lying in the river without a heart beating and without a breath that gave air to her lungs.

I shouted, 'Why did you kill her?' and I cried, 'Why did you roll her body into these sacks?' He denied that he had done it, and answered only, 'This woman worked against the government.'

I surrendered to the evidence that nothing would change. I asked permission to seek help from the arms of someone less fragile than me, to give my mother's body to the crows and eagles.[59] They denied me this. My mother was a separatist for them and no man with 'correct' ideas would touch her, unless I wanted my daughter to live what I had just finished living.

So I had to accept the help of my mother's murderer to give her the last farewell the following day. That night, my daughter and I slept hugging that waterlogged body.

Because of this, I decided to leave Tibet.

I made the trip with my daughter and my brother, who, a few years earlier, had decided to serve humanity with his prayers and become a monk.

After 18 days of travel and little food, we arrived in India. At that time, running away from China had not become so difficult. But our problems did not leave us in the new country. Everyone looked at us with suspicion, so much so that one day they called us spies and sent us back to the Tibetan border.

I did not resist and agreed to go to my native country, but on the condition that my daughter would stay and receive the teachings of His Holiness the Dalai Lama and grow up in the only place where she could learn her culture, remaining free to think, believe, and act like a real woman.

---

59. It was traditional in ancient Tibet not to bury bodies, let alone burn them, as it happens now, here in India. A corpse was cut into pieces and fed to other beasts in order to serve as nourishment for other beings and to continue the wheel of life.

I think that on the border with Tibet, the Indian police realized that there was a mistake in branding us infiltrators who worked for the Peoples' Republic of China.

After we were handed over to the Chinese, we were not allowed to return to our village but were escorted to a work camp, where we remained for three years. The name of this place is Tsari.

Everything that has happened since the Chinese began to claim Tibet is paradoxical.

I remember that my childhood was happy. I received honours that only a few had. My uncle was the aide of Ngari Rinpoche,[60] a high Tibetan lama who is also a brother of His Holiness the Dalai Lama, and due to this I could walk Lhasa's lingkor[61] with Ama Jetsuen Pema.[62]

I cannot say I had an unfortunate life. From the time of the arrival of the Chinese, it was not easy, but before that I had fortunes that only a few had, although everyone would wish they had them. I would be ungrateful if you considered me unlucky.

After my years in prison, my daughter, now an adult, wrote a letter requesting that we be reunited. She pretended to be ill and declared herself in need of maternal care. She requested that I come to India and take her back to Tibet.

This little deception worked.

Once again I embarked on the journey into exile. This time, I did not do it illegally. A good Chinese man with power

---

60. *Rinpoche* (in Tibetan: རིན་པོ་ཆེ་) means 'precious one' and is a term of reverence used for reincarnated Buddhist masters.
61. *Lingkor* literally meaning 'circumambulation', a clockwise route around a holy place.
62. The sister of His Holiness the Dalai Lama, the face and head of all TCV schools, she is the mother of all Tibetan children in exile.

within the government gave me an entry visa to Nepal. I arrived without any problem. That was the last time I saw my mountains, and now, I've been here for too many years.

My daughter got married to a Tibetan man who lives in America. She is also there. I am here alone, old and sick, and they still do not give me the visa to go to my family. My only hope is to be admitted into the retirement home which has been built outside the temple.

Last year, while at the Kalachakra, I fell and hurt my knee badly. I had to have pieces of iron put inside my body. Cleaning the house is difficult. My left leg is not the only difficulty that I deal with daily, I have other problems. Preparing food is boring if you have to eat alone.

But I try to take delight in life and its beauty. I do it by walking and looking ahead. I cannot stand straight because my back does not allow me to.

She laughs.

Twice in the past few years I went to Delhi, to the American Embassy, but on both occasions they denied me a visa. The second time they rejected all requests because an angry man broke a glass in the waiting-room office after receiving news that he would not obtain a visa again.

I am old, unlike you, and I have learned that life never denies anything to anyone. It seems to do so sometimes but it's just an illusion of our unrealised and frustrated desires. I thought about why my destiny worked against my plans to reach the USA. It did this for my long-term happiness. If I had left this place, it would be like going to prison. I do not know the language spoken in America. I would not be able talk with anyone. There are no monasteries. I could not pass, like I do now, several hours of my day praying and walking in sacred places. I would be far from His Holiness the Dalai

Lama, and I would not have his blessings in the last years that remain of this life and, for me, he is everything. He is the day and night of this world. If it was not for him, who would have allowed us, the common people, to have a new chance in a country that is not ours? Thanks to him, there is more compassion on this earth and certainly more love.

My only concern is what will happen if someone does not stop China. Not only for my people, but for all the nations that share borders with them.

When I was in Tibet, I remember a book in which Mao's desire was reported. Its content was the same as what I fear and what I have just said. I pray that this never happens. I do it only because I believe in peace and freedom for all sentient beings.

I do not think the Chinese are a bad people. They suffer as much as we do, and some of them fear that this will happen as much as I fear it. I do not know if it's true, but I've always believed that the old president of China did not die of natural causes. It is said that he was very attached to his physical appearance and went to a place to cure his baldness very often. One day, he was not able to return to his house after the medicines. A woman, whose name is said to be Chanche, poisoned him to put an end to the nightmare of the Cultural Revolution and to prevent the whole world from falling under its rules and under its control.

But my concern does not lead me to stop praying for my country to be free. Praying is the only thing that I can do at my age. I also pray that people stop working just for money and start collaborating with justice and truth. For the rest, I can only advise you to live trying to do good to others. If you are not able, you could cause evil through your actions, so stand still and do not act. Everything is a circle. Every action has a reaction that comes back to us with the same *intensity and violence with which it left us. It is karma that teaches us that it will respect our lives only if we respect those of others.*

If all people understood this, peace would be what we would have in return.

Our afternoon, meanwhile, flies. We accompany this old lady till outside the temple, with her reproaches, walking by the side of the road. She stops in a makeshift shop in the field beside the dark asphalt where the cars run. She buys herbs for her evening soup and bids us hastily. Her mind is now focused on her shopping.

Burning in the Fire

It is six o'clock in the evening and I walk through the streets of McLeod Ganj. In the distance I hear what might seem like a song to those who do not recognize the words. It's actually a prayer called 'Words of Truth'. I look around. I had not realized that all the shops were closed. I had arrived at the start of the event that had just begun.

I understand. We have reached the 170th self-immolation case in Tibet. I have commitments, but I abandon them. I follow the procession and I too start to speak the words of the music.

I remember the 47th case which occurred a little less than a year ago.

He was 23 years old. His name was Chopa. He was the son of a family of nomads, and the fire engulfed his body at ten o'clock that morning in the main street of Meuruma, a city in the province of Ngaba, a region located in the north-east of Tibet.

The intervention of the Chinese forces was immediate. They extinguished the flames instantly from the body of the young man completely burnt, yet still alive. The boy was transferred to a ghost hospital—its location and the doctors employed there are not known.

Hundreds of soldiers blocked the information coming from the hot zone with the usual method of cutting the telephone lines and not allowing anyone to travel. Restaurants and other Tibetan shops, voluntarily and due to the danger of repercussions, decided to remain closed as a sign of solidarity.

There was no other news besides this comment:

> *The history of Tibet has never seen a single case of immolation before the Chinese occupation. This tragedy would not have taken place if all Tibetan people had equal rights—political and economic—and were masters of their own lives. Unfortunately, it is the only alternative we have left to express ourselves.*
>
> —*Nyma T.J.*

Tenzin Tsundue

This is a different story from the others. It tells of a man who can hardly be described. He is the one who the *New York Times* identified as the new and better-known face of the Dalai Lama's boys.

I noticed him for the first time in the prayer held on 10th July, 2012, for the self-immolation of a boy. He had been the last to speak over the loudspeaker, and even on that occasion his words had been harsh and rugged.

Over time, I started to understand who Tenzin Tsundue is through the words of other people. He is one of the Tibetans most visibly engaged in the fight for an independent Tibet, and perhaps this is why his manner is so abrupt. Or maybe it is thanks to his unmalleable character that his tenacity in the struggle is so inflexible and incorruptible.

For this story I decided to follow his will—no trivial details which mention of the name of his mother or of the schools he attended. These pages will follow his will and his nature. Through gleanings from books that he himself published, I will tell the story of the rebel-poet of the new generation of Tibetan refugees.

Tsundue was born of the second generation of refugees who decided to leave the land of snows to follow their spiritual leader in exile. He was born in India but does not have the citizenship of this country.

He calls himself R, to mark his non-belonging to any country. He was born in Manali but his family lives in Karnataka. He studied in Ladakh, Chennai, and Mumbai. His sister lives in Varanasi, and his brother is with him in Dharamsala.

I am a foreigner living in India. My citizenship is Tibetan. It is a pity that Tibet is no longer on the maps. I like speaking in Tibetan, writing in English, and singing in Hindi—but my accent is completely wrong.

In short, I'm an R—a refugee—because when you are born and grow up in exile, this factor becomes a part of you and characterizes every aspect of you. I cannot call the country where I have always resided my home, and I understand that I am different from the people who populate this land. But I do not have any other place to call home. In the birthplace of my fathers, there is no place for me, except in prison. Yet in my heart I know that my home is there—that valley where my grandparents had a big farm and my parents played with the yaks.

But maybe I'm wrong too, to call myself an R. I'm a refugee, but if I study the Indian statute I understand that I'm actually a foreigner. India did not sign the International Refugee Convention in 1951 or the refugee protocol in 1967.

The Indians call me 'chinki', and the Chinese, when they arrested me, after having beaten me, they chased me off Tibetan soil saying, 'Out of here, Indian blood!'

I speak four Indian languages, I love Bollywood, and I have more Indian friends than Tibetans. My identity card bears the title, 'Certificate of Registration'. It says that I am a Tibetan national guest. So why does Tibet not exist for India? Why do they only recognize China? Who am I?

I grew up with the idea that the only thing I could afford was a room. I like rooms, the more spacious the better. They're where I can live, a home. They taught me that for us, home is a sacred dream reserved for a distant future. That's what really pushed me to become an activist. I want that future to become the present.

But before starting his fight, Tenzin Tsundue wanted to see with his own eyes what was happening in his land. Breaking all the rules, alone and on foot, he crossed the Himalayas to get to the forbidden land of Tibet. Here he was arrested and detained for three months in a concentration camp near Lhasa, where he experienced Chinese batons and torture devices. Beaten and thrown out of Tibet in 1999, he took the path of activism, joining the group Friends of Tibet, of which he is currently the general secretary. This is a commitment that, for him, was not only about distributing leaflets. In January 2002, during the visit of the Chinese premier Zhu Rongji to Mumbai, Tsundue climbed 14 floors of a building to hang a Tibetan flag and write 'Free Tibet' at the height of the room where the man from China was holding a business conference.

When I was a child, my parents left me with my grandparents one night to go to a nearby village to watch a movie. In response to this I broke the water pipe. My intent was not to make an aquarium of the kitchen, it was to get a reaction. This was my first act of protest.

When the elder official of the enemy state came to India, there was only a desire in my head to shout, 'Out of my country!' How could I do it? Only by showing it to him.

I climbed 14 floors of the Oberoi Tower, where Zho was holding a conference with Indian officials. I hung a red banner saying 'Free Tibet' and, while waving the Tibetan flag, I shouted slogans of freedom.

The prime minister was looking at me in the eye. In a moment, all the blinds of the windows in the room in which he sat were drawn. I was proud of my action, even though I had to stay in custody in the police station for 14 days. It was not an unpleasant stay. The Indian police sympathizes with our cause. Their minds are fresh and quick to seize the favourable points from the strategic side—if Tibet becomes free, Indian borders will return to being safe and trade relations with China will be less characterized by suspicion and fear.

In those days, I put all those feelings in black on white, in a cell in the prison of Dharamsala, and this is what this act gave me:

I was tall

Like Everest;

I have climbed Everest

And I was tall;

And my hands

Finally, free.

From that time, every time Chinese officials visit an Indian city, Tenzin must spend those days under surveillance, as demanded by the Peoples' Republic of China. He was one of the promoters of the march known as *Return to Tibet* in March 2008, during the Olympics that Beijing was hosting. He speaks of this experience:

The time for me to return to my land had come. Eleven years later, I walked towards Tibet again. Again, without permission. Why would I need a paper to be allowed to pass by the state that has not only occupied mine without reason, but is destroying it and leading it only through military intimidation?

I took part in a march to return from Dharamsala to my Tibet. The march started on 10th March, 2008, from the seat of the Tibetan Government-in-exile. We were to walk for six months to reach the Tibetan borders. Tibet and India share 4,075 kilometres of border. On the way, we cooked and camped in tents.

The past has already seen similar actions, but at that time we all worked with twice the strength we had, and I had a great hope for success—so much so as to donate the only possessions I had in this life, a small collection of books, to a bookshop in McLeod Ganj.

The march was peaceful, with a total absence of acts of violence. It was a sadhana, *a spiritual tribute to truth and justice, for which we were struggling.*

That was our long march, the march of freedom.

The day he set off, he left these few lines:

I say my last prayers and I begin my journey towards Tibet with more than a hundred companions—mostly monks and nuns, some laymen of my generation, and the elders who give us inspiration.

Even if the Indian or Chinese police try to stop us, we will resist.

See you in a free Tibet.

On the same date the march started, 50 years earlier, Tibet's capital had witnessed a great revolt against the foreign government. At that time Tibetans all over Tibet protested, calling for independence.

On the way, we found places where people offered us food and hosted us to sleep in schools, others gave us water, which was a precious gift.

The Indian militia escorted us with jeeps and motorcycles from district to district, until in the province of Kangra, on 13th March, we were arrested and held in prison for 14 days. I was called to a court hearing at the end of March and another in June.

How could they think this would be enough to distract us from our struggle? How many sisters and brothers in Tibet died that day, to cry out for our rights? How could we forget their sacrifice by surrendering?

On 19th April, we gave new life to the march. We were the same companions with the same ideals, but we left from a different point of departure—Delhi.

We woke up at four in the morning and started walking. During the day we covered about 25 kilometres over six or seven hours. We knew the Indian police would look for another pretext to stop us; if it failed, the Chinese would resort to guns and death. But the march meant more to us than its dangers—it was our chance to return home, make our voice heard, and probably some day live freely in Tibet. Whatever happened, we would not break the vow of non-violence. We would be beaten, tortured, and maybe killed; but we would never give up. I like to keep the Buddha and Gandhi in my mind and in my heart.

The Dalai Lama was asked, 'Can you end this madness?'

He answered 'No. I cannot. I have no magical powers.'

The *Return to Tibet* march failed to achieve its purpose. The marchers were stopped on the borders by the Indian police, who probably saved them from death at the hands of the Chinese.

What Tsundue believes is the reason for all the self-immolations is perhaps the one that satisfies me the most, among hundreds of other answers.

The protest of self-immolation was born in 1963 with Malcom Browne's black and white image—a monk covered in flames during the Vietnam War. For a Buddhist it is forbidden, whether by suicide or murder, to take a life. It is even worse if the life you choose to take is that of a human being, a sentient being. Since 2008, the Chinese Government has reached degrees of brutality that are too difficult to bear. Self-immolation is a desperate act of protest. But I live in India and for this I have no moral right to even be able to reflect whether it is legitimate or not.

He started publishing his books in 1999. With money borrowed from a friend, he published *Crossing the Border*. His second book, *Kora*, now in its eighth edition, has sold 20,000 copies. *Semshook* is in its third edition, and *Tsengol* is his last book, published in March 2012.

He frequently publishes articles in all the newspapers of India and on the 'Tibet Writes' website.

I pay my homage to this poet-activist, who is not very friendly, difficult to manage, but who deserves great respect for his ideas and for the magnificent way in which he expresses them on paper.

Bö Gyalo! Victory to Tibet!

His Holiness the Seventeenth Karmapa

Words can't describe the emotions I felt when my eyes met his, when he was right in front of me, when he placed the silk *khatag*⁶³ around my neck, when he gave me an envelope inside which there were the precious and rare pills, when he asked how he could help me, when he sat cross-legged in front of me, when he gave me his pen because mine started to run out of ink, when he invited me to stand by his side for a picture that will immortalize that morning at the beginning of September. I think this experience is one of those that I find so difficult to put into words.

I am not sure if I can succeed in expressing my feelings properly. When I close my eyes and try to recall the experience, I feel its subtlety and intricacy, and how deeply it touched me can never be represented through my limited descriptions. So I have decided not to report him directly, like I did with the others earlier.

Therefore, I will pass on his answers to my questions as if I was telling a dear friend a beautiful dream that I had a few nights ago, not using the precise words that

---

63. A *khatag* is a silk scarf, generally white, woven with the design of the eight lucky signs of Tibetan Buddhism and mantras. It is said that to receive a blessing, an object that acts as a means of receiving energy is necessary. The *khatag* and the knotted red cord are means for this.

I heard, but assuming that it was an unreal story.

An Italian lady reminded me of what an honour it was to start so young to be in the presence of such special personalities. I agree with her completely after this meeting.

In my heart I have an old but a very strong dream. I wore a blue *chupa*, a silk *khatag* around my neck, and in front of me stood a tall young man, with skin darker than mine but much brighter. His eyes, compared to mine, were smaller but much more intense. His head was shaved and he wore red robes. I was barefoot but the ground did not appear cold. It would have been the wood or the carpet with which it was covered, but for me at that moment the whole room was emanating the warm sensation you have when the universe embraces you in a big hug.

Of these moments, I remember these words:

There is a karma that overpowers us and makes us what we are. It is neither a destiny chosen by others nor a casual fate. We have created it and we keep it alive by feeding it with our own decisions and actions.

This belief is well-rooted in the Tibetan people. So, despite being driven to extremes difficulties in life, Tibetans accept the idea of karma, and can live with the fact that they are refugees. They seem to understand why their brothers and sisters get tortured and killed for remaining true to their identity and for their unflinching faith and devotion to His Holiness. Although China may have temporarily succeeded in controlling the Tibetans, it has miserably failed to win their hearts and faith. Contrary to what Beijing claims,

Tibetans find it difficult to live their life peacefully as they had been for centuries until China came to Tibet uninvited, under the guise of liberation. Many Tibetans get frustrated and some even opt for an extreme and a sad way to change the situation—self-immolation. Burning your body in fire, sacrificing your life, is so sad. But we empathize with those who have sacrificed their life for the greater good.

Life is a sacred gift, and even more so if it is the life of a sentient being. Why throw it into the flames? There are no results after such renunciation. It is time to put an end to methods such as these that sacrifice our precious human life. Prayer is slower and courage to resist is harder, but it is the right path to follow.

What we are experiencing as a people is the result of karma created by past actions. One of the characteristics of human beings is to err, and we do it very well, especially when very strong pain engulfs us. The mind, if not trained in the discipline of thinking correctly, makes mistakes. Among them, there is the mistake of not distinguishing the Chinese people from their government.

This type of error is lethal in many ways. First of all, if we get used to not making this differentiation, then we will no longer be able to think critically and truthfully, but will nurture feelings of anger and hatred towards our Chinese brothers, although they too suffer like us, although for different reasons. We fail to understand that the Chinese themselves are living in great suffering—lack of freedom, eviction from their land for a transfer to the highlands occupied by the state of Beijing—with climate and living conditions absolutely distant from their needs, and therefore dangerous for their health. It is impossible for them to have a balanced lifestyle. There is forced abortion and many other politically sensitive issues that constantly deprive them of a peaceful life.

This is reality, but due to lack of proper understanding, it is sad that Tibetans usually do not make a distinction between the common Chinese people and their government, the PRC.[64] When a Tibetan in Tibet says *gyami*, the term seems to refer to both the Chinese people and their government, whereas ideally, *gyami* means the Chinese people and *gyanag* means China. Seeing the Chinese people and China in the same light is a huge mistake because just like the Tibetans, millions of Chinese are also not happy in the PRC.

All this will end sooner or later.

Everything is cyclical and everything dies. With the life of humans fleeing away, so too is true of all the things created by them, whether they are objects or institutions. Democracy will be reborn from the ashes of torture and genocide, to blossom into a new era of peace. In China itself, something is changing.

The only reality that can live forever is the truth, and its holders have to do nothing but to wait for it to prevail, continuing to live in the right way.

Sometimes we have all the possibilities, but they are difficult to embrace.

In life we always have a choice, but it is simply easier to believe that we do not have it.

---

64. Peoples' Republic of China

Conclusion

This experience instilled in me a new understanding that, despite the pain and the tragedy, Tibetan culture gives birth to such strength in the people that it enables them to live their life in peace, just like they used to in free Tibet, when the sun shone brightly on them. Their indefatigable belief in the truth provides the energy to withstand huge sufferings and speaks clearly of the message that despite all odds, life must continue with more determination and courage.

Now I understand why life wants to live, because despite everything, this life is only a tiny segment of our lifetimes, and that by living it with a good purpose, we shape our future lifetimes.

27th January, 2018
New Delhi

With the image of a dream, this university project ended. With a moment of the magic of the oneiric, intertwined with the reality of moments that now reside only in memory, I came to the first truth of my life, which then became the thesis that I argued, through these interviews, in the classrooms of the University Statale di Milano—*Life Wants to Live*.

With a dream, this book ends and in the six years that separate me from the first draft of these pages, I dreamed, and dreamed strongly. I have lived, and I lived intensely. I consumed myself, starting from the love that the courage of these people has inspired in me, in their culture, their philosophy, their language, their myths and their superstitions. I dived in with all of myself into a magic without equal, and I wanted to be able to stay there forever.

My karma, however, after creating links and huge bonds with the footprints of these giants living in minute bodies, has torn me from this world that I now remember with affection and a tear of melancholy.

I am grateful to have walked the story of emanations of compassion, to have received their hugs, to have listened to their words, and to have prostrated myself before them, to have served them in the small way that this humble life could.

I give thanks for the knowledge that has been given to me, and I do it with every particle that constitutes me.

I will leave you with a piece of writing from years ago, when these moments were not yet memory.

7th April, 2015
Dharamsala

I grew up in Italy, dreaming about a mountainous land where I could hear the sound of trumpets and deep voices at prayer.

I grew up in Italy, but my spirit grew up in a Tibetan society.

I carry an Italian passport, but my family taught me what it means be a refugee.

I have been separated from my home since my teenage years ended and I finally decided who I wanted to be. I took the last flight, and I stopped this life to travel in the Himalayas.

Here, surrounded by my teachers and new family, I understood that all my trips around the world were not giving me what a single day at home here is able to give me.

And I learnt. I learnt, and I learn every day, and I will take ten thousand lifetimes to learn all the wisdom they have preserved.

It's a knowledge different from what Western countries usually teach you. It's not about the outside world, it speaks about the inner one.

It's pure spirituality and compassion.

It's pure clarity and life.

It's to learn how to not take yourself so seriously.

It's to accept your own mistakes.

It's to feel compassion for those who hurt you and pray for them.

It's to accept what happened to you because you have caused it (the evil and the good).

It's to transform yourself if you want the environment around you to change.

It's to devote good feelings to everyone, the people you care about and the strangers, too.

It's to learn how to prostrate yourself, because pride and the ego are the real enemies of happiness.

It's to learn how to turn the red prayer wheels with mantras written in pure gold. They carry thousands of sacred, secret, mantras and they always have to run in a clockwise manner to enter inside you and all around the environment.

It's to learn how to grow into a higher-level human being, not care much about money or the status or position when it comes to the practise of compassion.

It's to be involved, which requires love and compassionate values.

It's to learn how to dry the tears of others before your own, because we carry the key to not let them fall, and maybe someone else doesn't.

It's to accept that if there is a problem with a solution, it's useless to worry about it; and if there is a problem without a solution, again, it's useless to worry about it.

It's to make yourself understand that to kill even a mosquito is an evil action because even that mosquito has a life and life is precious, if not for you, for it at least.

It's to learn to avoid doing what you would not like others to do to you.

It's to make your heart full of this sentence—*If you cannot benefit or help others, at least try to not hurt them.*

My soul grew up in that land where high mountains preserve a non-violent society, where green hills are painted with thousands of prayer flags of all the bright colours I know, which dance all day and all night with the cold wind, where people shave their hair and wear red and yellow robes, where the temple is everything, where their status is just R and where the fact that others took away their land, name and rights is manageable. Intruders in their land can torture their bodies but will never be able to touch their minds.

Tibetans still have their dignity even after losing everything of their world. They still know how to smile from the heart, because deep inside, they know they are not the real losers, because from the perspective of the law of karma, they are not the perpetrators of all this. And they know that their *beloved leader, His Holiness the Fourteenth Dalai Lama of Tibet, blesses them every day.*

If you want to know something about me, learn about the Buddha's people, learn about the land of snow.

At that time I did not yet know that my life also wants to live, and that one cannot escape from one's own destiny. I hoped that this hiding place in the high mountains was my final destination. Unfortunately, it was not to be. How many tears I shed, the first nights far away from that place! How many tears before making peace with the acceptance of a path that should not end in that place! How many tears before understanding that this was the starting point of my life and not the point of arrival!

Now, years later, finding myself close to the point of preparing my suitcases once again and starting over again, starting a new cycle, I smile, reminding myself of that moment of apparent separation.

I have never really left the land that gave me my life back. There have been magnificent encounters, even stronger connections, which will never fade.

I thank you for your ability to dream; I thank you for the faith in the unknown; I thank you for the guidance, for the blessings, for love, and strength, and courage; I thank you for making me rediscover the spark that I could not grasp was inside me.

Now I am ready, full of gratitude, to let go of a huge piece of my life and, in an act of faith, to begin again.

This time I do it with a smile for the fullness that I carry inside and for another beautiful project that my heart has long wanted to do with you.

Because life wants to live, and I want to live with it.

Bibliography

Written Bibliography

- *Kora*, story and poems by Tenzin Tsundue, published in 2002 by Choney Wangmo, Delek Hospital, Dharamsala, India.
- *Semshook*, essays on Tibetan freedom struggle by Tenzin Tsundue, published in February 2007 by Tibetan Review — Tibetan Writers, Dharamsala.
- *Tsen-gol*, story and poems of resistance by Tenzin Tsundue, published in March 2012 by Tibetan Youth Congress, Dharamsala.
- *My Land and My People*, the original autobiography of His Holiness the Dalai Lama of Tibet, by Tenzin Gyatso, published in 1962 by Warner Books.
- *The Tibetan book of Living and Dying*, by Sogyal Rinpoche, published in 1992 by HarperCollins.
- *The Hundred Thousand Songs of Milarepa*, scripture 1135.
- *Thang Tong Gyalpo*, scripture 1485.
- *Il fuoco sotto la neve di* Palden Gyatso edizione Sperling & Kupfer, 1997.

Spoken Bibliography

- All people who spent time telling me their stories, about their lives, and who gave me permission to publish it.
- The Tibetan community who taught me their rites, language, customs and habits.
- Ven. Geshe Ngawang Sonam La, a translator of His Holiness the Dalai Lama.
- His Holiness the XVII Karmapa.

Wandu

Zomkyi

Dicky

Sonam Dicky

Ven. Bagdro

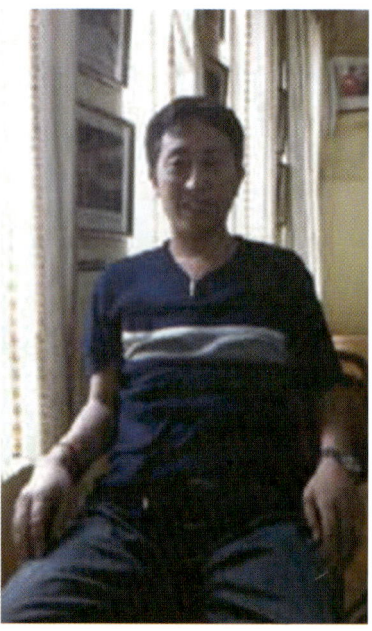
Phuntsok Wangdu

Tenzin Lhaky

Thang Tong Gyalpo

Milarepa

Tenzin Tsundue

HH The XVII Karmapa- *2012*

A pinch of my Tibet

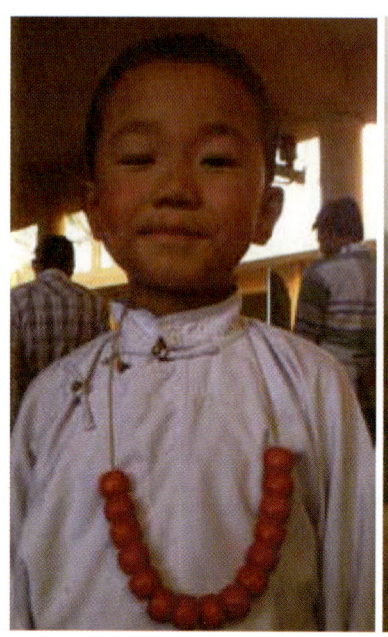

A special thanks…